I'M NOT THERE

21ST CENTURY FILM ESSENTIALS

Cinema has a storied history, but its story is far from over. 21st Century Film Essentials offers a lively chronicle of cinema's second century, examining the landmark films of our ever-changing moment. Each book makes a case for the importance of a particular contemporary film for artistic, historical, or commercial reasons. The twenty-first century has already been a time of tremendous change in filmmaking the world over, from the rise of digital production and the ascent of the multinational blockbuster to increased vitality in independent filmmaking and the emergence of new voices and talents both on screen and off. The films examined here are the ones that embody and exemplify these changes, crystallizing emerging trends or pointing in new directions. At the same time, they are films that are informed by and help refigure the cinematic legacy of the previous century, showing how film's past is constantly reimagined and rewritten by its present. These are films both familiar and obscure, foreign and domestic; they are new but of lasting value. This series is a study of film history in the making. It is meant to provide a different kind of approach to cinema's story—one written in the present tense.

Donna Kornhaber, *Series Editor*

I'm Not There

Noah Tsika

UNIVERSITY OF TEXAS PRESS ✦ AUSTIN

Requests for permission to reproduce material from this work should be
sent to:
    Permissions
    University of Texas Press
    P.O. Box 7819
    Austin, TX 78713-7819

♾ The paper used in this book meets the minimum requirements of ANSI/
NISO Z39.48-1992 (R1997) (Permanence of Paper).

Library of Congress Cataloging-in-Publication Data

Names: Tsika, Noah, 1983– author.
Title: I'm not there / Noah Tsika.
Other titles: 21st century film essentials.
Description: First edition. | Austin : University of Texas Press, 2023. | Series:
    21st century film essentials | Includes bibliographical references and index.
Identifiers: LCCN 2023006242 (print) | LCCN 2023006243 (ebook)
    ISBN 978-1-4773-2859-0 (cloth)
    ISBN 978-1-4773-2837-8 (paperback)
    ISBN 978-1-4773-2838-5 (PDF)
    ISBN 978-1-4773-2839-2 (ePub)
Subjects: LCSH: Haynes, Todd—Criticism and interpretation. | Dylan, Bob,
    1941—In motion pictures. | I'm not there (Motion picture) | I'm not there
    (Motion picture)—History. | I'm not there (Motion picture)—Influence. |
    Biographical films—History and criticism. | Motion picture industry—Law
    and legislation.
Classification: LCC PN1997.2.I464 T75 2023 (print) | LCC PN1997.2.I464
    (ebook) | DDC 791.43/72—dc23/eng/20230522
LC record available at https://lccn.loc.gov/2023006242
LC ebook record available at https://lccn.loc.gov/2023006243

doi:10.7560/328378

Contents

I'M NOT THERE

Prologue

Flaming Quotations

The British media theorist Rob Coley reports that when he first attended a screening of Todd Haynes's *I'm Not There* (2007), the film melted in the projector. At first, the accident seemed part of the work itself—an extension of its obsessive reflexivity, and yet another allusion to the European and North American avant-garde, to Ingmar Bergman's *Persona* (1966) and Hollis Frampton's *Nostalgia* (1971), both of which feature the destruction of the material substrate of photographic media. The failure—so extreme that spectators were left, initially, with nothing but silence and a white screen—immediately followed one of Haynes's clearest references to Federico Fellini's *8½* (1963): transmuted into a kind of human balloon, helium-filled and thus lighter than air, an already-otherworldly rock star rises to precipitous heights, his ankle tethered to the earth below by a long, limber rope. Haynes's film quotes *Persona* in a preceding scene depicting the character's mounting exhaustion. (Bergman's portentous tarantula reappears, along with his massive projections of human faces that ominously dwarf their living counterparts.) Scored to one of Bob Dylan's most enigmatic songs—the unfinished, occasionally unintelligible "I'm Not There"—the subsequent citation of *8½* also features the spoken words of a poet who, echoing an

A Felliniesque balloon.

interview that Dylan gave in 1966, says, "I know I have a sickness festering somewhere. I don't mean like Woody Guthrie,
wasting away in some hospital. I couldn't do that—decay like
that. That's nature's will, and I'm against nature. I don't dig
nature at all. The only truly natural things are dreams, which
nature cannot touch with decay." At the screening that Coley
attended, nature—materiality—intervened, much as Guthrie's
body had betrayed him by developing Huntington's disease.
Haynes's use of Fellini culminated, seemingly logically, in the
destruction of the celluloid itself.

Yet the literal decay—nature's will in the form of an over-
heated projector—functioned as an impetus for the imagination. After a moment's confusion, audience members received
it as a sort of confirmation of one of the film's key lessons regarding the limits of representation, the impossibility of biography. Haynes had liberated Bob Dylan, the film's ostensible
subject, from the shackles of the literal, and now the film itself
had been liberated from the screen. Unfinished, aborted—like
the title song, a dramatization of absence whose own conclusion is forever deferred, an emblem and agent of its author's

indecision—*I'm Not There* vanished phenomenally but persisted affectively, prompting Coley and his fellow audience members to contemplate the possibility "that there is no stable framework through which to encounter Dylan, but rather a multiplicity of cultural and temporal entry points." Instead of "bemoaning a ruined performance, then, [we] were roused to take up this performance [ourselves], to maintain its energy." Eventually, the audience "ceased to be an audience"; in its place were "inventors, perhaps even artists. Forging new, speculative connections as to what might be 'felt out,' beyond the frame of filmic representation, the group probed and transformed Dylan's ontology of 'untruth' into a means of collectively and reflexively engaging with the world."[1] Haynes—and maybe even Dylan himself—would have been pleased.

Excepting more recent works like *Dark Waters* (2019) and *Wonderstruck* (2017), *I'm Not There* is perhaps the least studied of Todd Haynes's films. In sixteen years, it has inspired little commentary beyond the burst of mainstream reviews that greeted its (limited) theatrical release. Auteurist investigations that aim for a certain comprehensiveness, like Rob White's book-length study of Haynes's career, cannot, of course, completely ignore *I'm Not There* (of which White is, incidentally, mostly dismissive). But the film merits attention for more than what it reveals of its celebrated director. Indeed, the film's title could even serve as a warning of sorts to auteurists. As Haynes once put it in a burst of extreme humility—or, perhaps, out of a sense of guilt for what could easily be construed as pure plagiarism—"I don't think there's anything in the script that's really my own."[2] Such confessions ultimately, however, indicate the extent of Haynes's literacy. "Although some writers will say 'I made it all up,'" observe John L. Geiger and Howard Suber in *Creativity and Copyright*, "such a statement is likely to reveal naivete and a lack of knowledge of the history of their art form."[3] "The Great sayings have all been said," Dylan writes in the liner notes to *Bringing It All Back Home* (1965). In repeating those sayings, artists like Dylan and Haynes test, and perhaps transform, the boundaries between plagiarism and adaptation, opening themselves up to legal challenges even as they benefit from certain jurisprudential shifts. "Once I understood what I was doing, I realized that I wasn't the first one to do it," Dylan writes in *Chronicles*. But he also acknowledges that "the legal and moral aspect" of homage has always "troubled" him, for it offers no easy answers.[4]

No study of *I'm Not There* can ignore the film's extreme allusiveness. What follows is an attempt to account for some of the artistic references and legal precedents on which Haynes builds his determinedly anti-essentialist opus—a biography that refuses chronology, disdains factual accuracy, flirts with libel, and cannibalizes Western cinema. That it can still be called biographical has much to do with Haynes's contractual ties to Robert Zimmerman (also known as Bob Dylan), who authorized its production and provided some forty songs. Indeed, *I'm Not There* has a complex legal history that the present study addresses in some detail. Bringing the law (specifically, copyright law, trademark law, and libel law) into conversation with Haynes's work allows for an expansive portrait of twenty-first-century cinema, and offers as well a sense of what made this obsessively citational biopic possible in the first place.

The book's opening section traces the origins and cultural significance of *I'm Not There*. The second section adopts a broader perspective to show how Haynes draws on Bob Dylan's long and complicated entanglement with the movies. The final section considers the promotion, reception, and "afterlives" of *I'm Not There*. In his 2010 history of the biopic, Dennis Bingham wrote, "Todd Haynes's tour-de-force exploration of Bob Dylan . . . may be the definitive statement on film biography for a long time to come."[5] Bingham's prediction has proved accurate: *I'm Not There* continues to influence filmmakers eager to avoid association with the less appealing connotations of the term "biopic," and it remains implicated in efforts to define the "appropriate" (or, at least, legally permissible) parameters of pastiche. Interspersed throughout the present volume are focused analyses of the adventurous film text itself. These close readings respect—and reflect—Haynes's nonlinear storytelling; they weave their way in and out of passages that endeavor to contextualize *I'm Not There* in historical, industrial, legal, and artistic terms.

I'm Not There offers what Jonathan Rosenbaum, writing about Tim Burton's *Ed Wood* (1994) and Quentin Tarantino's *Pulp Fiction* (1994), characterizes with the intriguing term "allusion profusion."[6] Denise Mann suggests that the effect of such vigorous bricolage "is to undermine any simple thematic resolution and instead to provoke a range of possible interpretations."[7] It is to such a provocation that this book responds, taking up the challenge of identifying and pursuing a multiplicity of references and interpretive approaches. "Who are you, Mr. Bob Dylan?" asks a French newspaper in Jean-Luc Godard's *Masculin féminin* (1966). Haynes does not answer (or even acknowledge) that question, but he certainly references Godard, as well as, for good measure, William Klein's *Who Are You, Polly Maggoo?* (1966). In Haynes's 2021 documentary *The Velvet Underground*, Lou Reed's sister, Merrill

Reed Weiner, warns him, "It is simplistic and cartoonish to think that there's an easy explanation." Ostensibly referring to her brother's behavior as a young man, her comment sounds a note of caution about the business of biography in general. It is a message that this book—the biography of a film—takes seriously as it roams among all manner of cinematic artifacts, leaps back and forth in time, and tries to show what provoked and informed a twenty-first-century essential.

Introduction
21st-Century Bedfellows

When Todd Haynes's *I'm Not There*, a resolutely eccentric account of Bob Dylan's art and iconicity, was released in 2007, many commentators made the quasi-biographical case for the filmmaker's close resemblance to his subject. Both men were said to be "mavericks" whose work had consistently resisted or recast convention—kindred spirits in creative subversion. If this equation between the famously gay Haynes, one of the architects of what B. Ruby Rich dubbed the "New Queer Cinema" of the early 1990s, and Dylan the legendary "ladies' man" seemed odd, it was offered as a way of explaining the fact that the typically uncooperative Dylan, who had a long history of thwarting attempts (cinematic and otherwise) to tell his story, had actually consented to, and thus facilitated, Haynes's efforts. Dylan must, many surmised, have seen something of himself in Haynes. The latter, noted David Yaffe, "came on the scene as the most audacious director of the New Queer Cinema, but like Dylan and the folkies, he could not be reduced to an ideology."[1] Several critics mentioned *Superstar: The Karen Carpenter Story* (1987), Haynes's famous experimental film, in which dolls bear the burden of representing the title figure's struggles with anorexia nervosa (among other ailments), as queerly consonant with some of Dylan's more outré efforts.

That *Superstar* is a passionate critique of the very patriarchal imaginary seemingly perpetuated through Dylan's often-sexist lyrics was something that no one appeared willing to concede at the time. Still reeling from the heady surprise of an authorized Bob Dylan movie (Haynes was the first director from the commercial realm of narrative fiction film to obtain the rights to Dylan's life and music), most critics simply settled for the sort of "psychological" interpretations that *I'm Not There* in fact avoids.[2] Attempting to account for the existence of a film that uses Dylan's own music and personae to unsettle biographical form, they ended up reverting to familiar biographical practices.

Even Haynes, promoting the film in the fall of 2007, engaged in some psychological speculation of his own when he said that "Dylan would never have wanted" to be the subject of a "banal, paint-by-numbers biopic." The evidence for this assertion could, Haynes maintained, be found in the fact that the icon had actually agreed to the filmmaker's "crazy-ass" idea to have multiple performers—including a woman and a Black child—portray various "versions" of "Bob Dylan," none of them bearing that name.[3] ("I have a problem sometimes remembering someone's real name, so I give them another one, something that more accurately describes them," Dylan writes in *Chronicles*.)[4] The project was to offer a complex interplay of transparency and opacity: in order to demonstrate that Dylan is decidedly "not there" in the film, Haynes would, paradoxically, be obliged to offer various invitations to find him. As in *Superstar*, which uses eleven unlicensed Carpenters recordings to counterbalance the status of plastic dolls as imprecise avatars (and which, as a result, was withdrawn from licit exhibition circuits in 1989, when Richard Carpenter and A&M

Records asserted their ownership claims), famous songs serve a clarifying purpose in *I'm Not There*. Dylan's music (both original recordings and covers) was always meant to pervade the film, as the sounds of the Carpenters pervade *Superstar*, and as David Bowie's work was to sonically structure Haynes's 1998 film *Velvet Goldmine* (whose very title is taken from a Bowie song, a B-side—copyright protection does not extend to titles). But Bowie, for whatever reason, did not want his music featured in Haynes's film. "It was very disappointing to me," Haynes admitted of the blow dealt by Bowie, "but he remained firm about his decision." As its title indicates, *Velvet Goldmine* would still boast abundant if indirect references to Bowie, leading Haynes to say, "I really hope Bowie can see in the film the affection and respect I have for him."[5] Haynes had, of course, every reason to so hope, given the tendency of stars like Bowie to threaten legal action against even pseudonymous depictions of their lives.

If the gender-bending, generally queer-receptive David Bowie would not consent to Haynes's planned tribute to the artist's Ziggy Stardust era, there was little reason to think that Bob Dylan would agree to let the director use Dylan's music or explore his personae in a motion picture. Haynes had, however, once described the two superstars in equivalent terms that celebrated their shared citational capacities. The Bowie of the early 1970s "was becoming a human Xerox machine," Haynes told Oren Moverman, with whom Haynes would later collaborate on the script for *I'm Not There*, "pulling constant references and recompiling them, condensing them, distilling them down into his own narrative diagram.... Everything ... came from somewhere else."[6] This, of course, is an apt enough description of Dylan, whose creative appropriations have ranged from the folk-approved to the reputedly plagiaristic. Haynes, too, is famous for his borrowings: the Oscar-nominated *Far from Heaven* (2002), perhaps his best-known film, pays tribute to the midcentury melodramas of Douglas Sirk as well as to cognate works like Max Ophüls's *The Reckless Moment* (1948) and Rainer Werner Fassbinder's *Ali: Fear Eats the Soul* (1974), reproducing their style with reverence and considerable attention to detail. Even *Safe*, Haynes's celebrated 1995 film, and the first of his works to feature actress Julianne Moore, draws on sources both high (Michelangelo Antonioni's *Red Desert* [1964], Chantal Akerman's *Jeanne Dielman, 23, quai du Commerce, 1080 Bruxelles* [1975], Fassbinder's *Chinese Roulette* [1976]) and low (*Poltergeist III* [Gary Sherman, 1988], the TV movie *The Boy in the Plastic Bubble* [Randal Kleiser, 1976]). Yet such reproductions—of style, mood, and tone—did not need to be licensed; Bob Dylan's music did. "There wasn't any way to do it without the music rights," Haynes has said of *I'm Not There*.

After consulting with Christine Vachon, his longtime producer and a cofounder of Killer Films, he decided that Dylan's permission would need to precede even the writing of the script; it was the chief condition of possibility for a project that Haynes had, by that point, only verbalized. His "checkered history with music rights," as he so euphemistically called it, made him understandably cautious. What's more, as a reader of numerous Dylan biographies—a devoted student of the star and his contexts (from the creative to the legal)—he understood that the attempt to do a film on Dylan represented "the longest shot" he'd ever taken.[7] "The one consistent problem I've had in my relatively short career," he wrote in 2006 while preparing to shoot *I'm Not There*, "has been getting music rights when the film I'm doing has anything even vaguely to do with a musician." Referring to his partnership with Vachon, Haynes added, "We've had doors consistently shut in our face regarding music rights when the artists felt they needed to exert control over what I was doing."[8] Indeed, copyright originated as a form of censorship, and that is precisely how it has often functioned for Haynes, whose *Velvet Goldmine* and *Superstar* clearly upset David Bowie and Richard Carpenter, respectively.[9] Without having to place explicitly censorial constraints on Haynes, Bowie and Carpenter could—and did—simply invoke copyright law, though their actions were certainly construable as attempts to stifle creative expression. (Carpenter in particular was possibly moved to respond not only to *Superstar*'s insinuations about his "private life" but also to the film's more insistent implication of the entire Carpenter family in Karen's ultimately fatal condition; Haynes had wanted to "redeem Karen's . . . image," to "rescue" her from "an incredibly . . . invasive family drama"—but invasive was, from the family's own perspective, exactly what the film seemed.) "In many ways, this conflict [between copyright and expressive freedom] has defined me as a filmmaker who can't get the music rights to his films and is, therefore, a guerilla," Haynes has explained. "And here I was thinking about the music rights of the most difficult, scary-seeming musical artist of them all. Dylan can sound tough—at times, scary-mean."[10] Countless writers have described him as such, and court records certainly substantiate this popular impression of Dylan as hardheaded and litigious. (He even parodies his own sue-happy reputation in Richard Marquand's 1987 film *Hearts of Fire*: playing a misanthropic rock star, he taunts the film's protagonist, a small-town singer who hopes to cover one of his songs, by saying,

"I'm gonna get some hot-shot lawyer in Nashville to haul your ass in court!") "He had," David Yaffe writes, "become notorious for wielding control of his image and was apparently waiting for someone to realize that one was not enough."[11] How else to explain that, rather than suing Haynes, Dylan was in fact helping the filmmaker?

Haynes's original subtitle for the project, "Suppositions on a Film Concerning Dylan," suggests its estrangement from standard biopics (while also echoing the title of Haynes's 1985 short *Assassins: A Film Concerning Rimbaud*). The first, plural noun indicates degrees of doubt, while the second preposition implies a certain distance from Dylan. This is not "The Life of Bob Dylan" or "The Bob Dylan Story" (the title of Andy Warhol's 1966 film, starring the East Village musician Paul Caruso in the title role, with Marlowe Duport as Dylan's then-manager Albert Grossman and Ingrid Superstar and Susan Pile as folkies) but a series of gestures toward the *idea* of making a Dylan-related film. (Martin Scorsese would find a kind of middle ground, subtitling his 2019 film on the Rolling Thunder Revue "A Bob Dylan Story.") From preproduction on, *I'm Not There* has been promoted—and received—as something other than a biopic. With "a premise counterintuitive to Hollywood orthodoxy," the film would "actually *celebrate* the impossibility of pinning down Bob Dylan."[12] "There's such anticipation for this movie because it's not a tired old biopic," claimed Haynes in the fall of 2007.[13]

Practical matters often contradict such expansive language. Dylan's "life rights" still had to be acquired in order to protect the production from its notoriously litigious subject.[14] Strictly in legal terms, then, *I'm Not There* is as much a biopic as, say, Michael Curtiz's *Jim Thorpe: All-American* (1951), which

Warner Bros. (where Haynes's maternal grandfather worked as
head of set construction) was able to make only after a years-
long bidding war for the rights to Thorpe's life.[15] (Neither denying the film's biographical credentials nor downplaying its
outré elements, Matt Prigge has helpfully suggested that *I'm
Not There* is best understood as a "*radical* musical biopic";
for her part, Kim Wilkins admits, "*I'm Not There* is certainly
a biopic, but by employing Dylan as its subject, it articulates
the problem with the representation of identity.")[16] Technically speaking, one's life story is not copyrightable—a lesson
that actor Gene Raymond learned in 1935, when, much to his
dismay, he discovered that, as *Photoplay* put it, "no one can
claim an option on the story of a man's life." (Raymond had
assumed that he was in possession of the rights to the life of
the composer and songwriter Stephen Foster, but a screening
of Joseph Stanley's Foster biopic *Harmony Lane* [1935], starring Douglass Montgomery in the role that Raymond coveted,
disabused him of that notion.)[17] But a life-rights agreement offers a certain degree of legal protection. By means of a "consent
and waiver" clause, it prevents a biopic's subject from suing
the filmmakers (whether for defamation, invasion of privacy,
or "commercial misappropriation"). It can also establish parameters for further cooperation between the two parties, as
when a biographical subject grants the use of personal archival
materials and other sources, including for commodity tie-ins
such as novelizations and soundtrack albums. The Hollywood
trade press began regularly reporting on the acquisition of life
rights in the 1930s, the decade of Raymond's rude awakening
about intellectual property. For Haynes, purchasing Dylan's life
rights seemed an essential step toward creative freedom, which
the agreement with Dylan essentially promised him. Doing

so was also a prelude to negotiating the licenses to Dylan's music, which, unlike his life story, *was* copyrighted. Various fees would need to be paid in exchange for synchronization and master-use licenses—the two rights that must be cleared for the employment of pre-recorded music in a motion picture; in the case of covers (of which Haynes planned to commission several), royalty fees would have to be determined by an impartial third party.[18] "I own the '60s," Dylan once told *Rolling Stone*, cheekily (though not necessarily inaccurately) conflating copyright and public history.[19]

Unprecedented in some ways and paradigmatic in others, *I'm Not There* made for a fascinating case study upon its release in 2007. It continues to offer valuable lessons about the legal lives (and reverberations) of commercial films, particularly biographical musicals—projects that must, almost by definition, negotiate multiple types of licensing. "Since the earliest days of cinema," write the editors of *Hollywood and the Law*, "legal instruments, processes, and institutions have influenced the conditions in which Hollywood films are made, sold, circulated, and presented."[20] *I'm Not There* vividly illustrates the idea that films are legal artifacts. (Its closing credits offer the following disclaimer: "This motion picture is fictional but certain characters and actions have been inspired by real people and real events.") Fashioned out of a specific set of binding agreements with Bob Dylan (who simultaneously pursued defamation and copyright infringement claims against creators other than Todd Haynes), *I'm Not There*, which quotes a wide range of cultural productions, also benefited from the courts' growing recognition of filmmakers' free-speech defenses.[21] Law professors Mark Bartholomew and John Tehranian have noted the courts' "increasing reluctance to stifle filmmakers' use of trademarked material," and it is this relative juridical largesse that allowed Haynes to pursue his pronounced referential passions even as other, less flexible legal frameworks constrained him (and required his backers to spend vast amounts for music rights). In contrast to copyright law, which, with its rootedness in a comprehensive federal statutory regime, necessarily structured Haynes's use of Dylan's music and of other forms of intellectual property, trademark law allows geographically separated judges more room for interpretation, as Bartholomew and Tehranian point out. *I'm Not There* thus illuminates the "seismic shift" that freedom of artistic expression has undergone in the twenty-first century, particularly in its entanglements with trademark law.[22] In 2022, Haynes himself described this shift and its potential to help rescue *Superstar* from the purgatory to which Richard Carpenter and A&M Records had consigned it. "There have been some legal opinions written about the film that seem favorable [and that indicate] a way through," he said, publicly acknowledging the changing legal landscape that had already tilted in his favor by the time he made *I'm Not There*.[23] Yet Haynes clearly understands that juridical conditions are less linear than, at best, pendular. Precedents can be ignored or invalidated; apparent advances can be nullified on a whim. Haynes admits that he once took antitrust legislation for granted, believing it to be forever secure—until, that is, the Reagan Justice Department disabused him of his youthful faith in such permanence.[24] It is unlikely that, in the United States in the twenty-first century, he will similarly presume his expressive rights are somehow guaranteed.

Fittingly, *I'm Not There*, whole sections of which reproduce the style and shot structure of Federico Fellini's *8½* (1963),

profited from a legal precedent—the so-called *Rogers* test—
that derives from one of Fellini's last films. Entitled *Ginger and
Fred* and released in 1986, the film tells of two aging cabaret
performers (played by Giulietta Masina and Marcello Mas-
troianni) known for impersonating the eponymous pair. The
actual Ginger Rogers, noting that she had not given Fellini
permission to use her name, promptly sued for trademark infringement. In 1989, the influential Second Circuit rejected
her arguments and affirmed Fellini's right to free expression,
establishing an important precedent from which Haynes has
benefited since *Poison*.[25] "In the end," write Bartholomew
and Tehranian, "[the defendants] won a seminal victory, re-
ducing the scope of trademark law and strengthening First
Amendment protections for artists."[26] The failure of Rogers's
$8 million lawsuit about a decade before the turn of the mil-
lennium heralded a new era in film history, one in which the
First Amendment rights of content creators like Haynes have
often trumped the intellectual property rights of trademark
holders such as the iconic Rogers. In the case of *I'm Not There*,
Haynes's right to express himself in the appropriated idiom of
8½ (among many other works) was greater than whatever consumer confusion might have been generated by the resulting
facsimile. (Rogers had contended that consumers would mis-
take Fellini's film for a product that she herself had endorsed;
she also feared that they would believe it to be a biopic rather
than an account of professional impersonation.) Haynes is,
of course, among the most citational of filmmakers; his work
relies heavily on brand imagery, including for the generally
well-protected purposes of parody and criticism. The *Rogers*
case occasioned a major shift that, by the time Haynes made
I'm Not There, effectively cemented an extremely low threshold

of "artistic relevance" for the kind of appropriative or otherwise referential work that he likes to produce. Some courts have even suggested that "the level of relevance [of borrowed trade marks and trade dress to a new work] merely must be above zero" in order for that work to qualify for First Amendment protection.[27] Clearly, then, Haynes was at least doubly fortunate: whatever his life-rights agreement with Dylan did not cover, the courts were exceedingly likely to protect. Who better than Todd Haynes to demonstrate the artistic relevance of trademarks used without authorization? Ask him why he chose to cite a particular film or figure and he will surely give you a detailed, disquisitive answer.

While dialogue, shot compositions, and characters (such as those purloined from *8½*) all fall under the scope of copyright law, the concept of fair use creates exceptions.[28] "Despite a common myth," Peter Decherney points out, "fair use is not measured by the percentage of a work used or by the number of words or minutes taken. Instead, work may be reused and reproduced without permission when the context has been significantly transformed and the amount of the work used is appropriate."[29] (In granting statutory permission to the public to make fair use of copyrighted material, the Copyright Act merely *suggests* that one consider "the amount and substantiality of the portion used in relation to the copyrighted work as a whole"; Decherney draws attention to the popular misperception that quantity necessarily determines protectability.)[30] In contrast to France, which recognizes an author's moral right to attribution, US law does not require that Haynes identify, say, Jean-Luc Godard by name in *I'm Not There*, though he quotes extensively from Godard's script for *2 or 3 Things I Know About Her* (1967), as when Charlotte Gainsbourg's

Claire, the French wife of Heath Ledger's Robbie Clark, requests a divorce.[31] "Language is the house man lives in," says a character in the Godard film, offering a gloss on Wittgenstein's philosophy. Borrowing Godard's own words ("I must listen, I must look around more than ever . . .") and placing them in the mouth of the introspective Claire, Haynes literalizes the Brechtian exhortation that *2 or 3 Things* invokes in its opening sequence: "Old man Brecht said it—that actors should quote." The speech that Haynes gives Claire comes from a moment that Martin Scorsese famously imitates in *Taxi Driver* (1976). In Godard's film, a character's contemplative utterances, delivered as voice-over narration, accompany a close-up of the swirling, bubbling contents of a cup of coffee (which becomes, in *Taxi Driver*, a glass of water in which a tablet of Alka-Seltzer steadily dissolves); Scorsese steals the image, Haynes the words. As David Yaffe speculates, "Haynes realized that rather than inventing dialogue for a realist Dylan, he could be freed by pastiche and come closer to his subject."[32] In *Creativity and Copyright*, Geiger and Suber offer an important reminder: "Copyright law is not simply limiting; it is also liberating."[33] For "you cannot copyright a convention," and, in any case, "evoking is not infringing." Indeed, "much of what is claimed to be copyrighted is not actually protectable by copyright law."[34] With *I'm Not There*, the ever-allusive Haynes would, however, test the limits of fair use by repeatedly engaging in what some courts call "literal appropriation"—the verbatim copying of dialogue (by, among others, Godard and Budd Schulberg), shot compositions, and more.[35]

He had, of course, done the same in earlier films. In *Velvet Goldmine*, for instance, Haynes copies a statement that

Lou Reed made to journalist Nick Kent in 1973, placing that statement in the mouth of Ewan McGregor's Curt Wild. McGregor's loose, slangy delivery introduces some minor variations, but Reed's words—unattributed—are reproduced almost verbatim: "I just think that everyone's into this [glam] scene because it's supposedly the thing to do right now. . . . You just can't fake being 'gay.' If they claim they're gay, they're going to have to make love in a gay style, and most of those people . . . just won't be able to make it. And that line—'Everyone's bisexual'—that's a very popular thing to say right now. I think it's meaningless."[36] Haynes admitted of *Velvet Goldmine*, "Virtually every line of the dialogue comes from something"—including Jean Genet's *Miracle of the Rose* (1946), which *Assassins* and *Poison* also quote. When pop star Brian Slade (Jonathan Rhys Meyers) is breaking up with his wife Mandy (Toni Collette), both parties speak the words of Oscar Wilde; inverted commas appear in Haynes's shooting script (and are perhaps detectable in the performers' ironic or otherwise distanced deliveries), but the status of these utterances as quotations (including from the novel *The Picture of Dorian Gray* [1891] and the essay "The Critic as Artist" [1891]) is not otherwise available to any viewer unfamiliar with Wilde's work. Elsewhere in *Velvet Goldmine*, Brian, at the climax of a fantasy sequence patterned on Max Ophüls's *Lola Montès* (1955) and the musical biopics of Ken Russell, declares, "Man is least himself when he talks in his own person. Give him a mask and he'll tell you the truth." Those, too, are Wilde's words. Brian reads them from cue cards that his assistant, the ambitious Shannon (Emily Woof), holds as if she were Dylan at the beginning of D. A. Pennebaker's *Dont* [*sic*] *Look Back* (1967). Dylan would himself appropriate Wilde's famous epigram, and seemingly attempt to pass it off as his own observation, in Martin Scorsese's *Rolling Thunder Revue: A Bob Dylan Story*.

With its countless derivations, *I'm Not There* ups the ante on these techniques. Like Dylan's, Haynes's thievery ranges from a benign allusiveness to what some might see as a "pathological kleptomania."[37] Throughout the film, his sources are used without attribution—a process that Greil Marcus has called "blind quotation."[38] Yet, as Decherney points out, the intensely subjective question of transformation, rather than the more empirical matter of measurement or naming, is central to determining the legal permissibility of such appropriations. The postmodern condition itself seems to militate against quantification. Jean-François Lyotard famously described it, and its characteristic bricolage, in terms of "the *high frequency* of quotations of elements from previous styles or periods."[39] The sheer density of allusions discourages attempts to police solely through enumeration. (Imagine having to add up all the citations in *Pulp Fiction*.) It was in 1990, just a few years after the publication of Lyotard's "Defining the Postmodern," that Second Circuit Judge Pierre Leval introduced the influential concept of "transformative use," effectively ushering in the "fair-use revolution" that has extended well into the twenty-first century.[40] As Decherney puts it, "Leval gave a name and theory to the changing legal interpretation of fair use"; he "successfully shifted the focus onto . . . the 'purpose' factor," which pertains to context and authorial intent (in other words, the question of how, where, and why, rather than simply what); finally, he "introduced a test that looked for ways that quoted works had been transformed in the new work, and he asked judges to consider whether the new work added value to the

original." Decherney demonstrates how Leval's transforma-
tive-use test gained influence in the 1990s, "embolden[ing]
fair use communities" and inspiring considerable judicial tol-
erance for the types of citations that Haynes likes to offer.[41]

In Martin Scorsese's *No Direction Home* (2005), Pete Seeger furnishes a telling analogy between the folk process and
certain legal patterns: "People take old songs, change them a
little, *add to them*, adopt them. . . . It happens in every other
field; lawyers change old laws to fit new citizens." Indeed, fair-
use doctrine—an altered understanding of copyright law, fashioned to suit new historical circumstances—would come to the
aid of Haynes on *I'm Not There*, sanctioning his many quotations and giving him the kind of "confidence and latitude"
that he needed.[42] The significance of the film thus derives, in
part, from how it illuminates its precise moment of production, a period that, in legal terms, is distinct in the history of
American cinema, and that differs from the climate in which
Haynes first started working. *Superstar*'s making (and legal
suppression) preceded the fair-use revolution. (Even Leval's
concept of "transformative use" was still years away.) In order
for that 1987 film to finally qualify for fair-use protections
more than three decades after its festival debut, Haynes will
need to annotate it, identifying every quotation and, as he put
it in 2022, "all of the sources of information and so forth."
Claiming "transformative use" requires, of course, scrupulous
identification of that which is being "transformed," and that
is exactly what Haynes plans to provide. "Yes, it'll happen," he
says of *Superstar*'s eventual legal sanctioning.[43]

The idea of "transformative use" would eventually be employed to defend Bob Dylan himself. The Princeton historian
Sean Wilentz (who, like Haynes, has enjoyed a privileged

relationship to the superstar) denounced the charges of plagiarism that, during the first decade of the twenty-first century,
seemed increasingly to hound this most referential of song-
writers. (The controversy was reignited in 2016, when Dylan
was awarded the Nobel Prize in Literature; posted the following year, Dylan's Nobel Lecture suggested that his unattributed
sources extended even to SparkNotes.)[44] "This isn't just a matter of law or ethics," Wilentz argued in Dylan's defense. "It's
a matter of the illusions we make in order to live, which is
one definition of art. Dylan, an artist, steals what he loves and
then loves what he steals by making it new."[45] In his book *Bob
Dylan in America*, Wilentz elaborates on the point, explaining that Dylan has consistently "assembled bits and pieces of
older American music and literature (and not just American
music and literature) and recombined them in his own way.
. . . But every artist is, to some extent, a thief; the trick is to
get away with it by making of [the stolen material] something
new."[46] What Wilentz is describing, whether wittingly or not, is
the legal category of transformative use, and his words apply
as much to Haynes as to Dylan. Indeed, the filmmaker has
clearly "gotten away with it" ever since the suppression of *Superstar*. Even widely publicized setbacks, like Bowie declining
to license his music to *Velvet Goldmine*, have not prevented
Haynes from operating as his own "human Xerox machine."

With its citational promiscuity, *I'm Not There* helped pave
the way for other, similarly literate works of cinema, like
Woody Allen's *Midnight in Paris* (2011), which Sony Pictures
Classics successfully defended against a lawsuit filed by the
estate of William Faulkner, and Rob Epstein and Jeffrey Friedman's *Lovelace* (2013), which the Weinstein Company, citing
fair-use doctrine, shielded from the copyright holders of 1972's

Deep Throat. (As the distributor of *I'm Not There*, the Wein-stein Company had plenty of experience with fair-use claims; Haynes has a tendency to keep attorneys and insurers exceed-ingly busy clearing his work as non-infringing before that work is disseminated to the paying public.) Allen, whose script included a nine-word quotation from Faulkner's 1951 novel *Requiem for a Nun*, was charged with violating both the Copy-right Act and the Lanham Act, which governs trademarks, service marks, and unfair competition. A Mississippi judge concluded that Allen had indeed "transformed" the Faulkner passage in his comic tale of time travel, adding "something new, with a further purpose or different character." (The judge, recognizing the value of homage, also wrote that literary allu-sion should be an object of celebration rather than litigation.)[47] Claiming copyright and trademark infringement, the owners of *Deep Throat*—over five minutes of which appear in *Love-lace*—sued to stop the release of the biopic (and also requested $10 million in damages), but a federal judge agreed with the Weinstein Company that "transformative use" had been made of the legendary pornographic film.[48] Yet if one of Haynes's goals with *I'm Not There* was to embrace opacity—to queerly preclude conclusive identification—then the film itself must be seen as nothing less than a limit case in the annals of fair use. For the determination of transformation depends upon precisely those ontological coordinates that Haynes evades or upends. It is impossible—legally unintelligible—in the absence of a clear conception of source material (such as that culti-vated by the inclusion in *Lovelace* of a clip from *Deep Throat*). Haynes, as Justin Wyatt suggests, constantly destabilizes his own points of reference.[49] In this, he is abetted by the sheer density of cinema history. The twenty-first century, in which the vast majority of his films have been made, is a dauntingly late date at which to invoke that history. No reference, except perhaps to a near-contemporaneous example, is unlikely to call to mind at least one intervening or intermediate text. This accretion of degrees of separation is most obvious in *Far from Heaven*, in which it serves as a structuring principle, such that each citation of Sirk is simultaneously a citation of Fassbinder, thus disrupting conventional notions of succession and revision. In *I'm Not There*, Haynes's quotations of *8½* often closely resemble *Stardust Memories* (1980), Allen's own gloss on the Fellini film. (Indeed, the hotel setting of many of Cate Blanchett's scenes closely mirrors that of *Stardust Memories*, and Haynes's chivvying superfans crowd the camera just like their counterparts in the Allen film—and, for that matter, in a manner that also evokes the ominous crowds in the "Horror" section of *Poison*.) Bob Dylan's allusive personae, distinct yet overlapping and inextricable (like the three sections of *Poison*), and presented in defiance of chronology, both symbolize and animate Haynes's challenges to copyright law.

Pursuing Opacity

If his ability to mine popular culture for its expressive potential was not stymied in an age of robust fair-use protections, Haynes still faced certain obstacles—legal, financial, and otherwise. Early on, he sent a one-page pitch to Dylan. It consisted of just two paragraphs, preceded by a pair of epigraphs: Rimbaud's "I is another" and what to Haynes had been a catalyzing line in Anthony Scaduto's 1971 biography of Dylan ("As he matured, he built a new identity every step of the way in order to escape identity"—which Haynes, incidentally, misquoted as "He created a new identity every step of the way in order to create identity.")[1] What followed, authored by Haynes, read: "If a film were to exist in which the breadth and flux of a creative life could be experienced, a film that could open up as opposed to consolidating what we think we already know walking in, it could never be within the tidy arc of a master narrative. The structure of such a film would have to be a fractured one, with numerous openings and a multitude of voices, with its prime strategy being one of refraction, not condensation. Imagine a film splintered between seven separate faces— old men, young men, women, children—each standing in for spaces in a single life."[2] Dylan's response, relayed to Haynes just a few months after the filmmaker first sent his pitch, was positive; *I'm Not There* could, Haynes felt, finally proceed.[3]

Was it pure luck? Or was there something specific in Haynes's approach (either promised in proposal form or achieved in the finished film) that appealed to Dylan, and that might hold lessons for filmmakers drawn to the exceedingly risky terrain of biography? Attempting to discern what Dylan "really" felt about the project, or about Haynes, would be a fool's errand. Certainly the film itself suggests as much—makes obvious, that is, the folly of ever accessing the "true" intentions of so mercurial an artist, for whom the very concept of intentionality may well be moot. Yet there are limits to such an exceptionalist approach. For Dylan may be no more of a shape-shifter than anyone fortunate enough to live out many decades—to live through tumultuous times. As Jesse Schlotterbeck suggests, *I'm Not There* is fundamentally about survival—about the privileged ability, hardly exclusive to Bob Dylan, "to keep both body and artistic spirit alive."[4]

A Dylan fan in his youth, Haynes conceived of the project while on a most Dylanesque journey—a cross-country road trip, undertaken in a "beat-up old Honda," from New York City, where he had lived for fifteen years, to Portland, Oregon, where he would eventually resettle.[5] (At the start of 1964, not long after *Newsweek* exposed him as a Jewish kid from the suburbs, Dylan made his own cross-country road trip, "a literal journey toward a psychic destination.")[6] It was January 2000—the start of a new millennium. *Velvet Goldmine* had recently bombed. Haynes was nearing forty and growing tired of the New York rat race. Traversing the continental United States, listening to scores of Dylan songs (from old favorites to those that he had never heard before), and reading some of the many biographies of the man, he hatched the idea for *I'm Not There*. But Dylan is a big subject, and Haynes, who had not worked with a cowriter since collaborating with Cynthia Schneider on *Superstar* some twenty years before, brought Oren Moverman in to help. At that point, the script was nearly finished, yet Haynes felt that he needed the sort of final push that only a close associate could provide. Moverman, because new to the project, was able to offer a kind of clear-eyed polish, an "objective" editorial eye.[7] In Haynes's telling, Moverman's most conspicuous contributions had to do with Dylan's Pentecostal period—the years during which, having "found Jesus," the Jewish artist underwent a full-scale religious conversion that extended even to his creative life, transforming him, for a time, into a gospel singer. (In an additional irony, the *New York Times Magazine* would describe Haynes's instructions to Moverman, a fellow Jew, as "Talmudic.")[8] The Israeli-born Moverman reportedly experienced something of Dylan's own "outsider's" fascination with Pentecostal Christianity. He read and listened to as much relevant material as he could, absorbing many of the lessons—spiritual as well as artistic—of Dylan's religious rebirth. As a result, the film's sole gospel number, performed during a relatively brief, documentary-style excursion into Dylan's Christian period, is something other—richer—than a mere parody of Pentecostalism. When Christian Bale's Pastor John, his hair in a rounded perm that lends him a striking resemblance to the painter Bob Ross, sings Dylan's "Pressing On," backed up by a Black choir, with John Doe's rich baritone pouring out of him, some of the emotional power of gospel music comes through.

After the shoot, Harvey Weinstein responded favorably to the "show reel," a promotional sampling of scenes that Killer Films had been circulating to distributors, and he acquired *I'm Not There* for release through the Weinstein Company, a

"Pressing On."

powerful studio that, in the wake of widespread allegations of
sexual abuse against its cofounder and chief executive, would
end up declaring bankruptcy in February 2018. As Haynes had
learned through his encounters with Richard Carpenter, A&M
Records, Mattel (the first copyright holder to threaten him
with a lawsuit over *Superstar*), David Bowie, and Bob Dylan,
ownership is a complicated, often erratic matter, subject to
personal and juridical vagaries. ("The law's a funny thing, ain't
it?" observes Kris Kristofferson's character in Sam Peckinpah's
Pat Garrett & Billy the Kid [1973].) Lantern Entertainment,
an independent film studio, was formed after its parent
company, a Dallas-based equity firm, acquired the assets of
the Weinstein Company during the latter's scandal-induced
bankruptcy auction. (It bought much of the Weinstein film
library—hundreds of titles, representing a major portfolio of
intellectual property—for $298 million.)[9] In 2019, Lantern En-
tertainment revived Spyglass, a company that had, beginning
in the late 1990s, enjoyed a five-year distribution arrangement
with Disney. (Spyglass's first film was M. Night Shyamalan's
smash hit *The Sixth Sense* [1999].) The relaunched Spyglass

Media Group, of which Lantern remains the majority owner, then acquired the Weinstein Company's film library. In the summer of 2021, the distribution rights to that library were transferred yet again, this time to Lionsgate, which, as part of the deal, took a 20 percent stake in Spyglass. Yet *I'm Not There* is among the more than two hundred "excluded titles" listed in bankruptcy court records, meaning that Spyglass has retained ownership of the film's North American distribution rights. Lionsgate might, of course, acquire those rights at a later date. Or it, too, might fold. In any case, ownership of *I'm Not There* will likely remain in a state of flux. (Even Dylan's songs have moved: in 2020, Universal Music Group acquired his publishing rights; a year later, Sony Music Entertainment gained all of his recording rights, dating back to 1962.)[10] Indeed, such uncertainty is a characteristic feature of commercial cinema in the twenty-first century, an age in which confusion and scarcity go hand in hand with increasing corporate concentration.

DYLAN ON FILM

Cinema has forcefully registered Bob Dylan's stardom and artistry from the very beginning of his career as a singer-songwriter. Pennebaker's *Dont Look Back*, which includes footage of Dylan's 1965 concert tour of England, is perhaps the best-known example, but Dylan himself turned to film directing in the late 1960s, including with the unreleased (and ostensibly uncompleted) *Bob Dylan's Circus Movie* (1967), a product of his *Basement Tapes* period, featuring Tiny Tim and Noel Paul Stookey.[11] He also directed the equally experimental documentary *Eat the Document* (1971), commissioned for a television series that was canceled before Dylan could complete postproduction, and *Renaldo & Clara* (1978), a nearly four-hour combination of concert footage and staged psychodrama that Dylan called his "first real film."[12] (Joan Baez was less generous: she called *Renaldo* "a giant mess of a home movie.")[13] More familiar is Dylan's appearance in Sam Peckinpah's revisionist Western *Pat Garrett & Billy the Kid*, an epic rendering of the historical clash between outlawry and officialdom in the latter half of the nineteenth century. He had a major role as a reclusive rock star in *Hearts of Fire*, in which he delivers such gnomic lines as "Stars are dead" and "No one ever shot me out of a cannon at the circus." Smaller parts followed in Dennis Hopper's *Backtrack* (1990, 1992) and in the unreleased neo-noir *Paradise Cove* (Robert Clapsadle, 1999). But the twenty-first century has seen a veritable explosion of cinematic interest in Dylan, starting with his Oscar-winning contribution to Curtis Hanson's *Wonder Boys* (2000), a shaggy comedy about a professor of creative writing (played by Michael Douglas) who is, as it were, struggling to paint his masterpiece (a second novel that has swelled to nearly unreadable length), and who reluctantly mentors a clever, cinema-obsessed student (played by Toby Maguire) prone to telling tall tales and, à la Dylan, inventing alternate personal histories. Dylan composed the film's theme song, "Things Have Changed," which he recorded in the summer of 1999, and which plays over the opening and closing credits, framing a feature that also boasts two "vintage" Dylan songs—"Buckets of Rain," from the 1975 album *Blood on the Tracks*, and "Not Dark Yet," from 1997's Grammy-winning *Time Out of Mind*.

In a promotional video for "Things Have Changed," which premiered in early 2000, Dylan performs the song while re-enacting scenes from *Wonder Boys*. New shots of Dylan in the role of Douglas's professor are intercut with actual clips from the film. At one point in the video, Douglas himself materializes in the role of Dylan and lip-syncs to the song, guitar in hand—a doubling that prefigures the many star-driven distortions and displacements of *I'm Not There*. Accepting the Academy Award (for Best Original Song) via satellite from Sydney, Australia (where he was on tour), Dylan thanked Oscar voters for their "boldness" in recognizing "a song that doesn't pussyfoot around or turn a blind eye to human nature"—a rather familiar bit of honoree bombast.

Dylan's Oscar augured a period of intense cinematic activity for the artist. In 2003, the Larry Charles film *Masked and Anonymous*, featuring an original screenplay by Charles and Dylan, was released. As in *Hearts of Fire*, Dylan stars as an eccentric rock icon—a barely fictionalized version of himself. As Roger Ebert (who gave the film just half a star) put it in his withering review, "Bob Dylan idolatry is one of the enduring secular religions of our day. Those who worship him are inexhaustible in their fervor, and every enigmatic syllable of the great poet is cherished and analyzed as if somehow he conceals profound truths in his lyrics, and if we could only decrypt them, they would be the solution to—I dunno, maybe everything."[14] This is precisely what *I'm Not There* avoids suggesting, though the film is not entirely dissimilar from *Masked and Anonymous*. (Both works boast a combination of original recordings and covers of Dylan songs; both feature a reporter who bedevils a Dylan figure; and so on.) As Penelope Cruz's religious fanatic says in the Charles film, referring to Dylan's musical output, "I love his songs because they are not precise—they are completely open to interpretation."

Released in 2005, the much-celebrated Martin Scorsese

documentary *No Direction Home* seemed immediately to re-
move the taint of *Masked and Anonymous*. In its interrogation
of "identity," it provided a template of sorts for Todd Haynes.
Many of the interviewees who appear in the film describe
Dylan's protean quality. "It wasn't necessary for him to be a
definitive persona," the Irish folk singer Liam Clancy says of
Dylan's development. "He was a receiver. He was possessed."

All told, *I'm Not There* took seven years to make. Haynes
called it his biggest undertaking—the PhD to his previous
master's theses.[15] To save money, the film was shot in Canada,
though Romania, a source of inexpensive, nonunion labor,
had been floated as a possible location.[16] (Line producer Guy
Louthan recommended that Haynes "shoot a large part of
[*I'm Not There*] in Eastern Europe . . . because labor is much
cheaper and the dollar goes a lot farther there. Also, a variety
of landscapes can stand in for other, more expensive landscapes.")[17] In the end, *I'm Not There* was shot in forty-nine
days in the summer of 2006, in some seventy locations in
and around Montreal—not as cheap as Romania, to be sure,
but still a bargain.[18] The specific geographical selection need
not seem arbitrary, a mere cost-cutting measure: as Michael
Denning points out, Dylan's Rolling Thunder Revue "was
not simply a U.S. tour; it crossed the border into Canada,
recruiting Canadian musicians and incorporating Canadian
settings and a little French dialogue."[19] (*Renaldo & Clara* even
includes the Montreal concert performance of Dylan's "Isis.")
Haynes, too, would make extensive use of Canadian talent on
I'm Not There; the film reflects the vibrancy of the Montreal
arts scene.

The shooting script bears the subtitle "Inspired by the life
and work of Bob Dylan"—a line that would undergo several

Montreal plays Manhattan.

curious permutations across the many promotional materials
for the finished film, suggesting the multiplicity and instability
that inform the Dylan myth. In the *New York Times Magazine*,
Robert Sullivan, who visited the set outside Montreal, said of
I'm Not There that the film "is as much about Todd Haynes as
it is about Dylan (or maybe even more)." Haynes was, Sullivan asserted, "doing his best to take the experimental into the
multiplex," much as Dylan had brought certain unorthodox
techniques into the musical mainstream. Rimbaud, a copy of
whose *Les Illuminations* (1886) appears in one shot in *I'm Not
There*, "seems to have inspired Dylan in his early days nearly
as much as he inspired Todd Haynes."[20] Such comparisons
between Dylan and Haynes are not uncommon. After Dylan
signed off on *I'm Not There*, he "never once interfered or even
inquired about the film," notes David Yaffe, "giving Haynes . . .
the kind of rare creative freedom Dylan enjoys himself."[21] The
result, like so much of Dylan's output, might seem inscrutable
to some. "Let's not bother with what it all means," wrote Sullivan. "No one on set seemed to know for sure; they all pretty
much trust Haynes that it means something."[22]

I'm Not There opens with a series of "mug shots" of all the film's Dylan figures—a rapid montage (repeated once) of six medium close-ups of as many characters, each one staring directly at the camera. Recorded over a period of about six weeks, the mug shots were carefully calibrated to match one another, much in the manner of their carceral counterparts, including so-called "suspect films"—brief moving-image records of incarcerated men made by American police departments (and a few private companies, like RCA, General Electric, and Universal) in the 1930s.[23] (Haynes's mug shots, whether by accident or design, also evoke the opening credits of the Warner Bros. crime drama *The Public Enemy* [William A. Wellman, 1931], which famously offer a criminological variation on the studio's typical introductory identification of characters and cast members.) Like his penal predecessors, who were committed to generating standardized visual records of prison populations, cinematographer Edward Lachman painstakingly positioned each of his subjects in the exact same location in relation to the camera. (Ben Whishaw, who plays a poet who goes by the name "Arthur Rimbaud," was the last of the six performers to submit to the procedure.)[24] The resulting montage suggests a certain sameness in difference (or difference in sameness). This is, in fact, the only sequence in which all six protagonists share a setting and are shot in an identical style. Early on, Haynes recognized that "each of [the main characters] would need a very different visual treatment," except when they are introduced as convicts. Drawing on the "intense range of styles" evident in the cinema of the 1960s (the decade in which Haynes chose to "root" the film), *I'm Not There* juggles various color schemes and gauges (8-millimeter, 16-millimeter, 35-millimeter).[25] But an equalitarian approach

Billy's mug shot.

reigns at the outset, when the Dylans are shown in rapid succession. Their expressions uniformly sober, the six figures nevertheless exhibit variations in height, age, race, and so on. Out of a single pose, multiplicity.

Kris Kristofferson's voice-over narrator names all six Dylans as the mug shots flash on the screen: "Poet, prophet, outlaw, fake, star of electricity"—and corpse (for the conceit of this expressionist prologue is that Cate Blanchett's "Jude Quinn," the Dylan of *Bringing It All Back Home* and *Highway 61 Revisited*, has died, perhaps in a motorcycle accident, and is laid out on a stretcher, to be wryly eulogized by the narrator). Haynes had wanted a woman to deliver the opening voice-over narration, as Janet McTeer had delivered that of *Velvet Goldmine*. But his top choices were unavailable. Eventually, however, it struck him that Kristofferson would be ideal, and not merely because of the star's personal and professional history with Dylan. Kristofferson, who recorded his narration remotely, without getting a chance to actually meet with Haynes, had the perfect gravelly voice through which to express a grizzled maturity.[26] Kristofferson's career

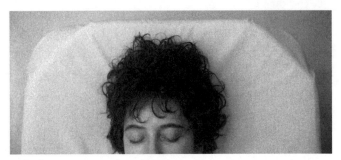

Quinn's corpse.

had periodically intersected with Dylan's. In 1986, the latter recorded a version of Kristofferson's "They Killed Him," which Kristofferson first copyrighted in 1983. In perhaps the most fortuitous convergence, Kristofferson was working as a janitor at the Tennessee studio where Dylan recorded *Nashville Skyline* in February 1969, and he was enlisted to hold the bongos and cow bell for drummer Kenny Buttrey to play during a take of "Lay, Lady, Lay."[27] The well-traveled Kristofferson had thus played his own part in Dylan's musical transformations; it makes sense that he would succinctly introduce these shifts in a film about Dylan's many selves.

The film's diffusive approach to "performing Dylan" certainly had its pitfalls, some of which were impossible to ignore by the fall of 2005—after the script for *I'm Not There* had been completed but before the start of principal photography— when the heavily ballyhooed Broadway production *Lennon*, in which nine individuals portrayed various "sides" of John Lennon, closed after just forty-nine performances. Approved by Lennon's widow, Yoko Ono, the show, which received scathing reviews, featured numerous Lennon songs and focused on the

artist's solo career, sidestepping the Lennon-McCartney cata-
logue (and its costs) altogether. Just as the dialogue in *I'm Not
There* would be drawn partly from Dylan's own utterances, the
book for *Lennon*, by Don Scardino, was based in the main on
various statements that the eponymous figure had made. Also
anticipating *I'm Not There* was the decision to cast diverse performers, including multiple women of color, in the title role.
"Everybody plays everybody," read the playbill—an approach
said to have been inspired by Lennon's song "I Am the Walrus"
(whose memorable first line is "I am he as you are he as you are
me and we are all together"). With its eccentric wordplay—its
sheer nonsensicality—"I Am the Walrus" would seem to inhibit
the very politicization that Scardino attributed to it, and that
he sought to express through the "inclusive" casting of *Lennon*.
Indeed, it would be difficult to call "I Am the Walrus" a clear
plea for "colorblind" practices—or, for that matter, for age- and
gender-neutral ones—just as it would be unwise to look for a
determinate "message" in the dispersion of Dylans in *I'm Not
There*. Indeed, "I Am the Walrus" has innumerable antecedents
of its own—everything from the writings of Lewis Carroll to a
British marching song from the Second Boer War.[28]

If the fall of 2005 brought the disastrous *Lennon*, it also
saw the release of the smash hit *Walk the Line*, James Man-
gold's account of the lives and careers of Johnny Cash and
June Carter Cash. (Reese Witherspoon won the Best Actress
Oscar for her portrayal of the latter.) For Haynes's backers, the
economic promise of a jukebox musical perhaps outweighed
the dangers of avant-gardism. Incidentally, Lennon and the
Beatles are shoehorned into *I'm Not There*. When Blanchett's
Quinn travels to London, he has a manic meeting with the
group, rendered in frenzied homage to Richard Lester's *A*

A hard Dylan's night.

Hard Day's Night (1964). Lester's work has exerted a conspicuous influence on Haynes, who quotes the Beatles film in *Velvet Goldmine* (when Brian Slade, like Ringo Starr, is asked, "Are you a mod or a rocker?"). At one point in *I'm Not There*, Haynes even re-creates, and embellishes, a famous image from Lester's *Petulia* (1968)—that of apparent whiplash victims, all middle-aged and wearing their finest attire (including, in one case, a custom neck brace), being wheeled through a hotel kitchen. (Haynes multiplies the victims—and the neck brace—for a scene in the distinctly Lesteresque film that Heath Ledger's Robbie Clark, the "star of electricity," makes in England; the title of that film—*Gang Plank*—evokes Lester's nautical thriller *Juggernaut* [1974].) There was also a more personal connection to Lester: Edward Lachman's longtime gaffer, John W. DeBlau, who served as chief lighting technician on *I'm Not There* (and who retired when the project wrapped), had been among those working to illuminate the Beatles as the Fab Four stepped off the plane on their first visit to the United States in 1964.[29]

Dylan is not, then, the only icon—or even the only rock

Franklin does Chaplin.

star—depicted in *I'm Not There*. Charlie Chaplin turns up, toothbrush mustache and all. Portrayed by the same Black child—Marcus Carl Franklin—who in other sections of the film embodies Dylan's own youthful emulation of Woody Guthrie, Chaplin appears in the guise of his most famous character, the Little Tramp. (It makes sense that Franklin, whose Woody is a freight-hopping "fake," reappears as the Tramp, for Chaplin's iconic costume, which he sought to legally protect, "invoked . . . real tramps, who rode railway cars and took odd jobs.")[30] Anxious, out of place and out of time, this Tramp clutches a ceramic statue of the Virgin Mary as he tumbles through the peculiar township of Riddle.

In his appearances as "Woody Guthrie," Franklin suggests the imitative flair that Dylan first exhibited in his migration from Minnesota to the eastern epicenter of the folk revival. Franklin's Woody is a runaway—an escapee from "a correctional facility in Minnesota." (Early on, Dylan was believed to have once been incarcerated in a juvenile detention center in Red Wing, Minnesota—the subject of his 1963 protest song "Walls of Red Wing.") A flashback shows the young Woody

reverentially listening to a Lead Belly record from the comfort
of an armchair in what looks to be a peaceful suburban home.
But the circus is passing by, visible through a window, and
Woody soon joins it. "It's lonesome roads we shall walk," he
later explains. After jumping into a river and nearly drowning,
Woody is rescued by Mr. and Mrs. Peacock (Vito DeFilippo
and Susan Glover), who take him to the hospital, then to their
well-appointed home. Feted by the Peacocks and their equally
adoring friends, Woody performs Dylan's "When the Ship
Comes In," which was first recorded in 1963 (some four years
after the scene takes place) and later covered by Arlo Guthrie.
(Franklin, alone among the leads, does his own singing in *I'm
Not There*.) After an ominous "official" telephone call mentions
"some state fugitive," Woody anxiously flees the Peacock home,
hopping the first freight that he finds (having failed to hitch a
ride in a truck). Dylan's performance of "Blind Willie McTell"
(based in part on "St. James Infirmary Blues") can be heard on
the soundtrack, faintly at first, blending with Woody's plain-
spoken monologue. "Now I'm just one walker that's stood way
up and looked way down across aplenty o' sights in all their
veiled and nakedest seasons," Woody says, staring out at the
passing landscapes. "Sightin' it, hearin' it. Seein' and feelin' and
breathin' it in. Suckin' down on it, rubbing it all in the pores
of my skin, and the wind between my eyes knockin' honey in
my comb." This monologue is, with minor variations (an extra
conjunction here, a missing one there, "suckin' down on it" re-
placing "sucking it down me"), a recitation of the actual Woody
Guthrie's much-admired description of the Pacific Northwest.[31]

Delivered in Franklin's amiable twang, the Guthrie passage becomes even homier—almost a "talking blues" number.
But Woody's fellow passengers—two old men (played by Don

Bound for Guthrie.

Francks and Roc Lafortune), seated on the other side of the boxcar, away from the open door—seem oblivious to its poetry. One is busy drinking from an old cup; the other just grunts. Woody, registering their disinterest, looks down. Cutting to a reverse angle, the camera zooms in on what he sees—a newspaper headline reading, "Famed Folk Stylist of Yesteryear Languishes Grievously in New Jersey Hospital." The article mentions the Greystone Park Psychiatric Center, the state facility where Guthrie, suffering from Huntington's disease, was housed from 1956 until 1961. The hobo's groan foreshadows Guthrie's catatonia, but the newspaper article seems to rouse everyone in the boxcar. The two old men, having glanced at it, look worryingly—or is it suspiciously?—at Woody, the Black child who goes by the name of the patient at Greystone Park. Woody avoids their eyes. Soon, he's hopping off the train, guitar in hand. He pivots to wave good-bye to the other men, who return the gesture; one of them even doffs his hat.

A bus takes Woody to Greystone Park (played—convincingly—by an imposing facility in Montreal). Brandishing a bouquet of red and white flowers, Woody visits his namesake.

The sight of the latter, lying motionless in a hospital bed, an oxygen mask resting on his chest, uneaten food on a tray before him, brings tears to the little boy's eyes. Suddenly, the patient's own eyes open; he catches sight of the child, who takes the opportunity to play a song. Visually, the allusion is to Dylan's 1962 "Song to Woody" ("Hey, hey, Woody Guthrie, I wrote you a song"), as well as to a similar moment in Arthur Penn's *Alice's Restaurant* (1969), starring Arlo Guthrie as himself, with Joseph Boley as the ailing Woody. But it is Dylan's much-later "Blind Willie McTell"—blaring now, a tribute to a different artist altogether—that dominates the soundtrack. (Despite relying on the melody of Guthrie's "1913 Massacre," "Song to Woody" is itself a joint salute: Dylan's lyrics mention "Cisco and Sonny and Lead Belly too.") This process of multiplication—a paean for Guthrie involving a salute to McTell—is a powerful reminder of the plurality of Dylan's influences. (It also resonates with the dual tribute to Sirk and Fassbinder in *Far from Heaven*.) Haynes even enacts this fecundity with some of his actors. In Hal Ashby's *Bound for Glory* (1976), an adaptation of Woody Guthrie's semi-fictional account of his life, the same actress—Melinda Dillon—plays two separate roles. In *I'm Not There*, Marcus Carl Franklin appears as both Woody and the Tramp. Peter Friedman, too, plays dual roles: he is both a folk expert who serves as a talking head in a television program on Rollins and a denizen of Riddle who peddles pamphlets purporting to tell of the township's downfall. The pamphleteer promises that his "epic tale of blunder and despair, a withering saga of mystery unveiled," is, in fact, "a swan song to America before Chaplin set sail." This eccentric invocation of Chaplin as a kind of explorer, akin to Vespucci or Ponce de León, is typical of Haynes's attraction to temporal rearrangements. His bold embrace of anachronism lends *I'm Not There* an irresistible insouciance.

MUG SHOTS AND MOVIE STARS

In his early coverage of *I'm Not There*, Robert Sullivan attempted to disabuse readers of the notion that the film would necessarily offer insights into Bob Dylan's life and career. "Todd Haynes's Dylan film isn't about Dylan," he argued, contradicting the voluminous advance press. (Much to his chagrin, Haynes's original, provisional subtitle, "Suppositions on a Film Concerning Dylan," had circulated widely, creating quite a stir and raising certain biographical expectations.) "That's what's going to be so difficult for people to understand," predicted Sullivan. "That's what's going to make 'I'm Not There' so trying for the really diehard Dylanists. That's what might upset the non-Dylanists, who may find it hard to figure out why he bothered to make it at all." Elaborating on the script's dialectic of visibility and invisibility, presence and absence, Sullivan wrote of Dylan's apparent passion for "changing, transforming, killing off one Dylan and moving to the next, shedding his artistic skin to stay alive. The twist is that to not be about Dylan can also be said to be true to the subject Dylan."[32] When, about a month after the publication of Sullivan's profile, Haynes was asked if he agreed with its title—"This Is Not a Bob Dylan Movie"—he answered with a firm "no," arguing that there would be little sense in denying the intimate connection between *I'm Not There* and its superstar subject (whose name, incidentally, appears throughout Sullivan's piece).[33] Gus Van Sant, Haynes's queer contemporary (and a fellow transplant to Oregon), had previously objected to attempts to position his 2005 chamber piece *Last Days* as a "Kurt Cobain movie" (despite having had star Michael Pitt made up to look as much like Cobain as possible), and his denials and deflections were part of a long Hollywood tradition rooted in a not-unfounded fear of lawsuits and related recriminations. (Cobain was dead when *Last Days* was made, but Courtney Love, his widow and the primary beneficiary of his estate, was very much alive; Love had even declined to participate in Haynes's *Velvet Goldmine* because of the uncanny yet entirely coincidental resemblance between Ewan McGregor, the film's star, and Cobain.)[34] When Haynes, for his part, took issue merely with the use of the term "biopic," he seemed to be resisting not accusations of libel but rather what he saw as the gaudiness of the genre—a cheapness that he parodies in *Superstar*, with its self-conscious behind-the-music framework. Yet in dismissing the *Times* title, Haynes would perhaps further complicate matters by simultaneously identifying a range of films as "Bob Dylan movies"—including those with which Dylan was in no way involved and that even preceded the 1961 publication of his first song.[35]

What might have seemed a rather fanciful hagiographic gesture—placing the all-powerful Dylan at the center of cultural productions that in fact predated his career—could also be viewed as a way of productively diminishing the man's singularity, of seeing antecedent works as pointing the way for his varied pursuits. In *Velvet Goldmine*, Toni Collette's Mandy Slade, looking back on the beginnings of glam rock, asserts that Jack Fairy was "truly the first of his kind, a true original." (That she resorts to redundancy—Fairy was *truly true*—suggests that she is not entirely confident about her historical claim.) "Everybody stole from Jack," she insists. Mandy's firsthand memory, unreliable in any case, does not, of course, extend to the days of Oscar Wilde, which Haynes briefly re-creates to imply that cultural lineages are often a lot longer than popular discourse allows. Calling Elia Kazan's *A Face in the Crowd* (1957) "a Bob Dylan movie," as Haynes did in 2007, was, perhaps, a way of suggesting that the "Dylanesque" can be found in some unexpected places—and *avant la lettre*.[36] Less anachronistic than simply an example of unbounded thematic analysis, Haynes's generous approach indicates the breadth of his film's concerns. "All of the lines in the film, let alone the settings and the scenarios, come from *something* in the Dylan universe," Haynes has said.[37] Yet the "Dylan universe" encompasses, for Haynes, much more than the man's own authorial efforts. Whatever its relationship to the term "biopic," *I'm Not There* places Dylan—as *Velvet Goldmine* places glam rock—in an expansive context, one that consistently accounts for important prehistories.

Rimbaud represents, of course, one such prehistory. Haynes had already explored aspects of it in his student film *Assassins*, which Joan Hawkins has described as "less about Arthur Rimbaud the real boy-poet than . . . about 'Rimbaud,' a character we have largely constructed from his writings and from the legends and myths that have grown up around him."[38] With its attention to the act of playing Rimbaud (one scene shows the film's lead performer attempting to "get in character"), *Assassins* anticipates the reflexive aspects of *I'm Not There*, in which a version of Rimbaud appears as a version of Bob Dylan. For Whishaw's scenes as the poet, Haynes would, appropriately enough, reproduce elements of *Assassins*, which also has Rimbaud (or, rather, the actor playing him) being interviewed while seated in front of a white wall. In *I'm Not*

There, the "quasi-governmental interrogation" that Rimbaud undergoes, and that provides the mise-en-scène for the mug shots of the other Dylan figures, was filmed in an abandoned warehouse outside Montreal, pitch-black except for the bright white light used to create a high-contrast quality. Visiting the set, Robert Sullivan was struck by this "white glowing light, like something in a dream"—this "bright blast of white light" that marked the "white-wall interrogation of a teenage poet."[39] The harsh lighting scheme evokes Andy Warhol's *Screen Tests* (1964–1966), a series of silent, static medium close-ups of various individuals whom Warhol and others instructed to stare in the direction of the camera while refraining from "acting."[40]

As an elaboration of the introductory black-and-white images of the six Dylan figures—a mug shot come to coquettish life—Whishaw's Rimbaud suggests a certain defiance of Warhol's injunction against "performing." ("Come on, man—direct me!" an impatient folk singer instructs a listless Warhol [Guy Pearce] upon submitting to a *Screen Test* in George Hickenlooper's 2006 film *Factory Girl*.) Waving his hands, fidgeting, smoking a cigarette and then stubbing it out, smiling, laughing, grimacing, flirting, Rimbaud challenges his offscreen interrogator while gazing directly at the camera. He seems, at times, to be interrogating the film's viewer as much as he himself is being interrogated. His gnomic remarks are issued as challenges; many seem to defy interpretation. Yet this Rimbaud is also a kind of choric figure, commenting on the characters seen and strategies enacted elsewhere in the film. As an always-seated onlooker, he shares the viewer's own immobile spectatorial position—a correspondence encouraged by the intimacy of direct address.

The visual style of the Whishaw segment seems patterned

Whishaw's Rimbaud.

on direct cinema, to an even greater degree than that of Blanchett's, which features a far sharper, lower-contrast black-and-white cinematography more evocative of certain heavily capitalized studio productions of the 1960s, the decade that also saw the making of *Dont Look Back*. While the latter film is clearly referenced throughout many of Blanchett's scenes, its look, like that of the grainy works of direct cinema that preceded it, is better approximated in Whishaw's appearance as a talking head. As cinematographer Edward Lachman recalled to the *New York Times Magazine*, Haynes "said that the obvious thing would have been to use the style of D.A. Pennebaker" for Blanchett's scenes. A less predictable approach, one that Haynes and Lachman ultimately employed, involved reproducing the look of Fellini's *8½* and *La Dolce Vita* (1960), among other European art films, via Kodak Plus-X 5231 and Double-X 5222 black-and-white negative stocks.[41] If Blanchett's Jude, pestered for insights into his creative process, recalls the Guido of *8½*, the very "versioning" of Dylan evokes *La Dolce Vita*, in which Anita Ekberg, Lex Barker, and even the young Nico all play "versions" of themselves, restaging their

La dolce Dylan.

established and emergent star personas for Fellini's cameras; Haynes also alludes to Ekberg's famous arrival by plane when he has Jude touch down in a London teeming with reporters and photographers.

Like the rest of *I'm Not There*, the Rimbaud sections are rooted in a heterogeneous documentary record—an archive that encompasses not only the poet's published letters (explored so extensively in *Assassins*) but also elements of the French Decadent movement (epitomized here, as in *Velvet Goldmine*, by Joris-Karl Huysmans's *Against Nature* [1884]) and, of course, Dylan's own interview responses and other public statements. In *I'm Not There*, Rimbaud's interrogation is based on actual court records. (The poet was questioned extensively after he was shot by his lover, Paul Verlaine.) With his tattered nineteenth-century ensemble—vest, coat, cravat—Whishaw's Rimbaud is a vision of prematurely decayed dandyism. The tangle of hair atop his head certainly suggests mid-sixties Dylan, yet the evocation of Warhol's *Screen Tests*— as much as the references to Rimbaud—complicates this iconic outline. The *Screen Tests* display, as Jonathan Flatley argues, "the radical instability of recognizability."[42] Famous faces (including that of Dylan, who sat for Warhol's 16-millimeter camera in the summer of 1965) are defamiliarized through proximity and duration—through "intimacy" and monotony. Warhol's radical approach to documentary portraiture sought to expose the impossibility of "acting natural" (itself an oxymoronic expression), and the concomitant strangeness of simply and continuously "being oneself." To scrupulously maintain "emotionlessness" is, of course, to perform. The *Screen Tests* thus question the logic of so-called "portrait films" (whether celebrity profiles or records of "ordinary" people), which promise, as Paul Arthur puts it, "to illuminate an irreducible core of being."[43] Filming Dylan, among hundreds of other visitors to the Factory, Warhol demonstrated the limitations—the inadequacy—of indexical images, the failure of the documentary form to reveal "essences." It is little wonder, then, that Haynes cites the *Screen Tests* in *I'm Not There*, his determinedly anti-essentialist opus.

Like other characters in the film, Whishaw's Rimbaud is *funny*. As Sullivan observes, the poet "weaves commentary and humor throughout the film," his witticisms sharpened by Whishaw's almost bitchy style of performance (which echoes everyone from Clifton Webb to Ed Hood, who offers caustic observations on a scene of seduction in Warhol's *My Hustler* [1965]).[44] *I'm Not There* is, in part, a comedy. As Haynes put it, Rimbaud, the film's de facto narrator, lends "a tonal lightness" while introducing a thematic of play. With Whishaw's swishy Rimbaud, as with Marcus Carl Franklin's Black Woody Guthrie (whose race is never mentioned), Haynes is "playing around with [Dylan] myths and letting you in on the joke."[45] Having worked with Haynes on *Velvet Goldmine*, Christian Bale told

the *New York Times Magazine* he was "prepared . . . for the
audacity of the script, for so many Dylans, so many different
kinds of films within one film." But he also emphasized the
comic elements of Haynes's work: "I started reading the script
. . . and I just started to laugh."[46] Bale's earliest scenes, in which
he portrays sixties protest singer Jack Rollins (the Dylan of
The Times They Are a-Changin' [1964], whose iconic album
cover is faithfully reproduced here), were shot in 16-millime-
ter black-and-white, using old Kodak film stock, as was Rimbaud's interrogation.[47]

Haynes introduces Rollins via a mockumentary that looks
back on the performer's career. The sequence begins by quoting the *New York Times* as calling Rollins "folk music's troubadour of conscience." In keeping with his expansive approach,
Haynes borrowed the term "troubadour of conscience" not
from any historical assessment of Dylan but rather from a 1998
profile of one of Dylan's inspirations, Pete Seeger. (Steve Curwood of *Living on Earth*, a weekly environmental news and
information program broadcast on public radio, called Seeger
"the *nation's* troubadour of conscience.")[48] Framed as an investigation into the "disappearance" of Rollins—into his "death"
and eventual "resurrection" as a Pentecostal Christian named
Pastor John—the mockumentary recalls similar sequences in
Superstar, *Poison*, and *Velvet Goldmine*, all of which involve
various forms of post hoc analysis. The postmortem is literal
in the case of *Superstar* but merely figurative in that of *Velvet
Goldmine*. In the latter film, the onstage assassination of the
David Bowie figure, Brian Slade, is revealed to have been a
hoax—as much of a simulation as the documentary investigations that follow, and that Haynes fashions, in part, in homage
to Orson Welles's *Citizen Kane* (1941). Documentary television

Alice and Jack.

plays a prominent role in *Velvet Goldmine*: news broadcasts and other nonfiction forms punctuate and comment on the narrative proceedings. Preparing to fake his own death, Slade himself watches a live feed of the avid fans gathered just beyond his dressing room. Throughout the film, television cameras capture the responses of such audiences, relaying them to one another as well as to the objects of their ardor.

I'm Not There offers a similar take on documentary media as vehicles of contact between artists and their audiences. "Jack Rollins, folk sensation of the early sixties, was the promise of a new generation," claims the narrator of Haynes's mockumentary, which furnishes evidence of the man's impact on young fans. "So what was it that made him run at the height of his career and throw it all away, trading in the limelight for a different kind of light altogether?" The mockumentary's layered soundtrack, in which the informative voices of interviewees elegantly blend with a recording of "The Times They Are a-Changin'" (the cover version, by Mason Jennings, via which Bale is dubbed), suggests a sonic dissolution of the boundaries between past and present that the program's narrator, with

Fabian's folk heyday.

her insistence on themes of departure and conversion, seeks to uphold. Julianne Moore's Joan Baez figure, Alice Fabian, says of Rollins, "He saw what was going on in the world, and he had the ability to distill it into a song." (Haynes will repeat this particular clip as if to underscore the mockumentary's resemblance to a recursive television program, the kind that inevitably circles back to claims included in a pre-credit précis.) Friedman's folk expert, also attesting to the talents of Rollins, gushes, "He could do a funny thing, he could do a pathos thing—he was sensational!" (He might be describing Haynes himself.) There follows an uncanny re-creation of Dylan's fidgety 1964 appearance on *The Steve Allen Show*.

Yet Rollins, like Dylan, is too big for television alone, and soon a movie is being made about his meteoric rise. "Today, the name 'Jack Rollins' might best be remembered as the tortured singer battling his conscience in the 1965 drama *Grain of Sand*—the role, of course, that launched the career of Hollywood rebel Robbie Clark," says the narrator (played by Jane Wheeler), introducing a sepia-toned clip of the Rollins biopic, in which Heath Ledger, playing Robbie playing Jack, smoothly

"GRAIN OF SAND" 1965

Robbie as the cocky Jack in Grain of Sand.

slings a guitar strap around his neck and announces with all the loftiness of a cocksure young star, "Hell, I don't pick what I sing—it picks *me*. Some of it ain't pretty! How are you ever going to change anything if you only want to show what's pretty?" He is lecturing a young woman who stands beside him in a recording studio, her head cocked, one hand on her hip and the other clutching a collection of papers. Her exact role is unclear; she could be a reporter visiting the young Rollins as he prepares to record (or is it Rollins who is the guest in *her* studio, as Dylan was at Cynthia Gooding's radio show *Folksinger's Choice* in 1962?); perhaps she is the star's assistant, or his wife. Registering his condescension, she sighs and looks away, seemingly exasperated by his sexism (which anticipates Robbie's own treatment of his wife, Claire). The clip also evokes *A Face in the Crowd*, particularly those scenes in which Marcia Jeffries finds herself ensconced in a radio studio with the restless Lonesome Rhodes.

The poster for *Grain of Sand*, shown as part of the program on Rollins, is closely patterned on that of the Kazan film (just as the poster for the Robbie Clark vehicle *Calico*, seen later in

Robbie's Jack, revived on television.

I'm Not There, evokes that of Sidney Lumet's *Serpico* [1973]). The sententious tagline for *Grain of Sand* reads, "The Voice of a Generation—who threw it all away!" In another clip, however, Robbie's Rollins is indicting not himself but an unnamed collective, saying, "They took away the meaning. . . . I was a pawn in their game." Is he referring to record executives, or (like Dylan in "Restless Farewell") to the folk purists? Pointing to a billboard promoting his new album, he complains, "It's not about *me* anymore—it's all about *him*." The face on the billboard is that of Bale's Jack Rollins—the "real" Rollins, the "original," the reason *Grain of Sand* even exists. When Claire, having divorced Robbie, catches the biopic on television some ten years later, it is this scene that she watches; it culminates with Robbie, as Rollins, looking directly at the camera—at Claire, at us.

Haynes fills *I'm Not There* with such examples of direct address. Perhaps most memorable of all is Cate Blanchett's final appearance as Jude: after reciting portions of Dylan's enigmatic response to a question that Nora Ephron asked him in a 1965 interview, Jude turns to stare at the camera, offering the faintest of smiles. The moment mirrors the ending of *Masked and Anonymous*, in which Dylan's Jack Fate glances at the camera from the back seat of a moving vehicle. On the soundtrack, Fate sums up his credo: "I was always a singer, and maybe no more than that. Sometimes, it's not enough to know the meaning of things. Sometimes, we have to know what things don't mean, as well. . . . Things fall apart, especially all the neat order of rules and laws. . . . I stopped trying to figure everything out a long time ago."

Violators Won't Be Cited

Like the Dylan works on which it draws, *I'm Not There* is germane to debates about the fine line between homage and plagiarism. (As Pauline Kael wryly remarked in her negative review of Woody Allen's *Another Woman* [1988], a virtual remake of Ingmar Bergman's *Wild Strawberries* [1957], "An homage, according to Peter Stone, is a plagiarism that your lawyer tells you is not actionable.")[1] Robert Sullivan puts it simply: "As Dylan stole song and lyric styles—from the Clancy Brothers, from Civil War poets—so [*I'm Not There*] cops different Dylan-era directorial styles."[2] Such penal language, which certainly resonates with the carceral inspiration for the mug shots of the six Dylans, is often joined with equally aggressive rhetoric to suggest that Dylan, in thieving, is also killing: Rob White writes of the man's "paradoxically self-multiplying rock 'n' roll suicides," much as Sullivan registers his penchant for "killing off one Dylan and moving to the next."[3] Distinguishing between "composed dialogue" (by which he means "original" lines written by Haynes and/or Moverman) and the quotation of "actual interviews," Sullivan attempts to offer a guide to navigating the film's pastiche. Dylan's 1966 interview with *Playboy*'s Nat Hentoff is the source of Jude Quinn's "In that music is the only true, valid death you can feel today off a record player," among other lines; Dylan's 1997 conversation with *Newsweek* editor David Gates supplies part of Billy's final voice-over narration: "I can change during the course of a day. I wake and I'm one person, and when I go to sleep I know for certain I'm somebody else. I don't know *who* I am most of the time."[4] (Much of Blanchett's final monologue, delivered from the back seat of a limo coursing through a nocturnal landscape, is also lifted verbatim from the Gates interview.) For Rob Coley, such quotations constitute "a good example of how Haynes's technique does not merely involve the repetition of . . . interview transcripts, but treats the words as a refrain which produces difference in the act of their repetition."[5] Here, again, is the concept of "transformative use": transposed from the printed page onto the silver screen, and from music journalism into dramatic acting, certain words seemingly assume new meanings.

Yet Haynes has said that, to him, Dylan's original interviews were already, on their own, theatrical. Reading the transcripts, he felt that Dylan's utterances represented "improvised performance art at its highest. . . . I remember thinking, 'This has to be re-enacted.'"[6] If "transformation" is the watchword for fair-use claims, mimesis is more likely to be pursued, and rewarded, in the realm of screen acting (which is not, of course, to discount the "transformative" dimensions of emulation, or the plaudits that stars so often receive for appearing, however momentarily, "unrecognizable," especially in biographical roles). Having won an Oscar for her studied imitation of Katharine Hepburn, Blanchett, who dutifully scrutinized Dylan's published interviews between takes, described to the *New York Times Magazine* her own hyperawareness of Haynes's citations. She spoke of "knowing that [the lines] reference . . . something that has already been said," of being "constantly aware [of] referencing primary, tertiary, and secondary sources—the whole Dewey system was crashing in on me."[7] Yet the film's viewer is not necessarily aware of these lines as citations. They are unmarked—quotations that appear without the cinematic equivalent of inverted commas or other tokens of appropriation.

The absence of textual identification makes *I'm Not There* a more extreme case than Haynes's earlier films, such as *Assassins* and *Poison*, which clearly cite their sources in credit sequences. The opening credits of *Poison*, for instance, include the words "inspired by the novels of Jean Genet, with quotations from *Miracle of the Rose*, *Our Lady of the Flowers*, and *Thief's Journal*"; the credits of *Assassins* similarly name the writings of Genet, Arthur Rimbaud, Paul Verlaine, Mathilde Mauté, and Paul Louis-Ferdinand Céline. By contrast, the opening credits of *I'm Not There* include only the words "inspired by the music & many lives of bob dylan" (his name pointedly decapitalized, as in his 1971 novel *Tarantula*); the closing credits list only the copyrighted music heard in the film—songs for which royalty and licensing fees were paid and compulsory, synchronization, and master-use licenses granted, along with a few folk ballads in the public domain. (Unlike those of *Bound for Glory*, however, the end credits of *I'm Not There* do not actually identify which of these works are in the public domain and which required licensing.) Nowhere in the text itself can one find any direct references to the published interviews, produced screenplays, and other works that the dialogue quotes (often verbatim). One must bring such knowledge to the film, or risk assuming that Haynes simply made it all up. (Trying to maintain the fiction that *Last Days* is in no way about Kurt Cobain, Gus Van Sant went so far as to say of the film's story, "I felt more comfortable just making it all up.")[8] As Joan Hawkins has written, Haynes's work "requires a certain amount of what Pierre Bourdieu calls 'cultural capital' in order to be fully appreciated. The sheer abundance of textual references . . . reward[s] . . . familiarity with both high art and high-end popular culture."[9] Recognizing this rather wide span, Rob White explains, "Haynes's allusions have varying degrees of directness. Sometimes the association is vague. . . . On other occasions, the incorporation is more like direct quotation."[10] Yet such straight lifts typically appear without attribution. In some instances, that is because Haynes didn't even know he was stealing: his plagiarism of *Petulia* was, he has said, entirely inadvertent—so "innocent" that he was able, at first, to think himself quite the pioneer. When he recounts this slightly embarrassing story in his DVD commentary, Haynes is characteristically charming. His confession is not merely self-deprecatory, however. It also resonates with the words of Eric Lott, from whom Dylan seemingly lifted the title of his 2001 album *"Love and Theft"* (the first and, to date, only of Dylan's album titles to be placed in quotation marks): Lott describes "musical melancholia" as a peculiar condition—a distinct psychic location—in which "you get by with materials you barely remember taking in the first place: you were too young, or they were too available, or both, and they work so well, speak so solidly to your condition."[11] *Petulia*, however inadequate Haynes's memories of it, proved indispensable.

Fair-use doctrine implies no need to inform the audience via in-text citation. Haynes, for his part, has spoken of his interest in "allowing breathing space for viewers" and "ma[king] them feel respected—that they [are] sophisticated and . . . able to locate meaning for themselves."[12] ("UNDERSTAND

WHAT YOU WILL," encourages an intertitle in Godard's
Masculin féminin.) Certainly, much has changed since the
days when Haynes made *Assassins* as an undergraduate at
Brown. Perhaps recognizing plagiarism as a specifically academic impropriety, Haynes diligently cited his sources—
including letters and diary entries—in that student film.
Though *Poison* retains elements of this citational practice,
Haynes has since dispensed with such onscreen identification,
leaving it to extratextual forms (press kits, reviews, fan web-
sites, interviews) to provide spaces in which obscure sources
can be acknowledged directly and discussed at length. (In
Dottie Gets Spanked, Haynes even includes, on an intertitle, an entire sentence from Freud's famous essay "A Child Is
Being Beaten," but he neither employs quotation marks nor
names Freud as the sentence's author; Freud's name does not
appear in the film's credits.) "When you were young," observe
John L. Geiger and Howard Suber, "you were taught to always
give credit to the author of something you took from another
source. But this is an academic rule, not the law of copyright."[13]
Peter Decherney concurs: "Plagiarism," he writes, "is a broad
ethical and professional category and not a strictly legal one,
though it does overlap with copyright law."[14] After *Poison*,
and despite (or as a result of) his legal run-ins with Richard
Carpenter, A&M Records, and Mattel, the now-experienced
Haynes seemingly accepted the difference between plagiarism
and copyright infringement—between an ethical question and
a strict liability statute—and he did not look back. In 2007,
he told Greil Marcus about some of the many sources from
which he "stole" for *I'm Not There*; they included "collections
of all of the [Dylan] interviews from '65, '66," which Haynes
once again described as "intensely dramatic, like transcripts

Mouthing Dylanisms.

of performance art—radical, creative, but lived performances that, to me, just screamed to be performed again. I wanted to hear them be performed aloud, I wanted to fill them with flesh again, and that also triggered kind of a creative urge. With all of the stuff brimming in my head, the ideas of the film emerged."[15] Mindful of the legal theory of transformative use, Haynes was "remaking" historical material, "adding value" to a published transcript by having the great Cate Blanchett recite it on the screen. From uncredited quotation would come something "fresh"—and certainly "cinematic."

After viewing an early cut of *I'm Not There* in the spring of 2007, an excited Haynes breathlessly told the *New York Times Magazine* that the film "is like nothing else." Harvey Weinstein would echo him, telling the same publication, "Nothing's ever been attempted like this before."[16] Both men were, perhaps, gilding the lily. For *I'm Not There* bears a striking resemblance to *Velvet Goldmine*: both films flirt with historical fiction and feature a mercurial musical artist who greatly offends young concertgoers by performing the "wrong" kinds of songs; both offer an eclectic mix of original recordings and covers commissioned by music supervisor Randall Poster; both concern obsessive journalistic inquiry into the permutations of a particular star image; and so on. (Haynes, too, clearly took considerable inspiration from *Masked and Anonymous*, itself a kind of Bob Dylan biopic.) There is, in any case, no requirement that a derivative work attain unparalleled status in order to qualify for legal protection; to "transform" appropriated materials is not necessarily to achieve singularity, whether in terms of classification or of quality.

What Haynes accomplished with *I'm Not There* is consistent with many of his broader efforts as a filmmaker. Promoting *Carol* in the fall of 2015, Haynes told critic Michael Phillips that, for him, making a film is always akin to making a mixtape.[17] "I wish I could show you what director Todd Haynes showed me," began Phillips's article on *Carol*, referring to the filmmaker's collection of the many images that had inspired him. "It'll never be published; it'd be a legal nightmare to secure the rights [to] its contents."[18] Yet, as Haynes understood when making *I'm Not There*, such materials are fair game for use in a motion picture. For *Carol*, Haynes and Edward Lachman re-created the work of photographers Saul Leiter, Esther Bubley, Ruth Orkin, Helen Levitt, and Vivian Maier, investing it with a libidinal energy that, in this tale of lesbian desire, effectively transforms it—"adds value" to it.[19] (Besides, as Geiger and Suber point out, evoking is not infringing.)[20] The degree to which Haynes's creative process parallels that of Dylan is striking. As David Yaffe notes, "Dylan has said that he stores up material in a box—containing snippets from books, movies, and probably conversation—that he dips into when he needs inspiration. . . . 'I didn't write that,' he [will] claim about a particular song. 'The box is writing the song.'"[21] *I'm*

Not There even dramatizes these parallels: Jude peruses issue after issue of *Life* magazine and, like Dylan in *Dont Look Back*, collects newspaper clippings, carefully forming his own editorial collage.

PLAYLISTS

I'm Not There repeatedly incorporates Dylan's own singing voice even as it relies on covers of his songs, until, at the very end, after a succession of stand-ins, the man himself appears, in a kind of reprise of *Superstar*, which culminates with the flesh-and-blood (or skin-and-bones) Karen Carpenter making a final, fleeting, chilling appearance.

Analogous to his use of cover songs are Haynes's re-creations of famous movie scenes. But just as he includes Dylan's own recordings, he also utilizes found footage—material filmed by others—including a clip of Dylan performing a portion of "Mr. Tambourine Man." Old images, like songs composed in the sixties, become new again—cropped to fit Haynes's widescreen aspect ratio.

An outtake from *The Basement Tapes*, the title song is audible at a moment of crisis for Jude Quinn. Its inclusion was a major coup: the film's soundtrack represented the song's first official release, after years of bootlegs.[22] "Here it is as much of a whirlpool as it ever was," writes Greil Marcus of the famously unfinished song, "but instead of capsizing a filmmaker's fables with its own supposed authenticity, it fades into the picture, nothing more and nothing less than one more story among all the rest."[23] It joins a number of other outtakes, demos, and alternate recordings, including an early version of "Idiot Wind" (1974). Lyrically, at least, this version is perhaps too congruent

Haynes closes the film with a haunting clip of Dylan's 1966 performance of "Mr. Tambourine Man."

with the celebrities-in-court sequence that it accompanies. Silent except for "Idiot Wind," the sequence, its visible participants muted, their words unavailable to the audience, opens with a judge handing down a decision. Robbie storms out while Claire celebrates. The two, viewed through an upstairs window in a voyeuristic high-angle shot, subsequently clash in the courthouse parking lot. Their respective attorneys attempt to intercede; their children appear confused, distressed. It is at this point that the song's opening verse can be heard on the soundtrack: "Someone's got it in for me / They're planting stories in the press." This, of course, is the rarefied complaint of a famous person—as famous as the Robbie glimpsed as if by the prying, spying paparazzi. Yet the congruence may be even deeper and more meaningful than that. For "Idiot Wind," which begins in the manner of Dylan's most accusatory songs, with vituperative charges being leveled at a detested "you," ends with the culpability of "we"—a resigned admission of shared responsibility. "You're an idiot, babe / It's a wonder that you still know how to breathe" becomes "We're idiots, babe / It's a wonder we can even feed ourselves." As Robbie and Claire quarrel over their kids, who are eventually wrested from their father—against their will—it may seem that both adults are, ultimately, to blame for the situation, as though there can be no winner in a divorce or custody dispute. Fittingly, this is not the jaunty, somewhat aggressive album version of "Idiot Wind" (which Joni Mitchell, for one, viewed as representative of the regrettable "masculinization" of the material for *Blood on the Tracks*) but an earlier, slower recording in a higher key, stretched to nearly nine minutes (though Haynes uses just a snippet—enough to establish its prevailing mood).[24] Mournful, almost a dirge, dripping with regret, it's the ideal accompaniment to the formal dissolution of a marriage. Yet it seems equally appropriate to the saga of Riddle, with which the divorce proceedings are intercut. As Dylan, on the soundtrack, laments the press's distortion of facts, Billy picks up a newspaper that identifies Pat Garrett as his captor and that reproduces a decades-old photograph of Billy—hardly an accurate index of his current appearance. It is then that Garrett and his entourage arrive—in cars that look like they are from the 1960s (or later). The lawman and his associates are swept into town on an idiot wind.

Equally notable are the Dylan songs that Haynes chose not to use, perhaps out of an awareness of their familiarity and close association with other filmmakers, like Richard Linklater, for whose *Dazed and Confused* (1993) "Hurricane" helps set the mid-seventies scene, and Cameron Crowe, who chose to conclude *Jerry Maguire* (1996) with the New York recording of "Shelter from the Storm." In Bernardo Bertolucci's heavily referential *The Dreamers* (2003), many of whose cinematic sources are directly cited via interpolated clips (Bertolucci seems to reserve unacknowledged quotation for moments of

Claire's day in court.

self-plagiarism, as when he restages the elevator scene from
1972's *Last Tango in Paris*), "Queen Jane Approximately" accompanies Michael Pitt's induction into a movie-mad club; it
would, perhaps, have been redundant to add it to the similarly
citational *I'm Not There*. "Just Like a Woman," one of whose
stanzas Shelley Duvall's *Rolling Stone* reporter delivers with
deadpan reverence in Woody Allen's *Annie Hall* (1977), appears only in eponymous form in Haynes's film—four words
that a frazzled but quickly recomposing Jude Quinn utters by
way of explaining feminine wiles (in a winking moment that,
meant to telegraph something of the eccentric process of artistic inspiration, comes perilously close to recalling the mawkish
manner in which, in Robert Zemeckis's *Forrest Gump* [1994],
a digitally manipulated John Lennon derives the lyrics for
"Imagine" in awed response to the title character's description of Communist China on *The Dick Cavett Show*; Haynes,
too, will manipulate historical footage, making it seem as if
Lyndon Johnson, his presidential image projected in tripli-
cate onto the white walls of a gallery space, is speaking lines
from Dylan's 1965 "Tombstone Blues"—"Death to all those who

would whimper and cry" and, paraphrasing somewhat, "The sky isn't yellow, it's chicken"). Another Dylan song—"See You Later, Allen Ginsberg," from *The Basement Tapes*—is cited only in dialogue: Quinn's sidekick, Sonny (played by Joe Cobden), utters the title in punning reference to the poet's departure, perhaps planting the seed. Also absent in *I'm Not There* is anything that Dylan recorded after 1997. Though acknowledging the aging process through Richard Gere's anachronistically named Billy the Kid, the Dylan of *I'm Not There* is resolutely youthful. The film's closing image, borrowed from *Eat the Document*, is of the man himself, looking no older than the middle-class students who, seen standing in their peacoats and penny loafers in the film's penultimate shot (also borrowed from *Eat the Document*), gather to watch him perform. Dylan's late-career rasp enters the soundtrack, via "Cold Irons Bound" (1997), as Quinn, having vomited in the aforementioned gallery, is ushered into a limo. But it's mostly his much-younger voice that is heard in *I'm Not There*.

Certainly, Dylan's sheer longevity would have made a more comprehensive historical treatment difficult if not impossible. In any case, *I'm Not There* is characterized by the lack of inclusion of any definite post-seventies developments (unless one counts the documentary on Jack Rollins/Pastor John, patterned, Haynes has said, on the PBS of the 1980s, though it culminates in a depiction of an early church performance of "Pressing On," which Dylan debuted on the gospel circuit in 1979).[25] Perhaps the reason has something to do with Haynes's own predilections—his pronounced, consistent interest in periods that predate his debut as a maker of feature films. That Haynes is very much a specialist in period pieces is a point that is often underemphasized—lost, perhaps, in a legitimate sense of his queer-theoretical acumen, his apparent embodiment of a specifically postmodern sensibility. Yet nearly all of his films are careful re-creations of the past, not just cerebral reflections on "pastness." Joan Hawkins, writing about *Assassins*, which excavates the 1870s and places that decade in a dialectical relationship with the film's own moment of production in the mid-1980s, emphasizes Haynes's "extreme attention to period costume and décor."[26] Rob White speaks of Haynes's "resistance to naturalism," but such an interpretation, however justified by the formal experimentation and high-theoretical élan of so many of the man's films, tends to ignore their grounding in scrupulous forms of historical reenactment.[27]

Is there a better evocation of the eighties than the aerobics scene in *Safe*, in which a Lycra-clad Carol White cavorts to Madonna's "Lucky Star"? Every detail is period-appropriate. This is no Brechtian quotation—no resolutely antinaturalist distillation of an idea. To suggest otherwise is to undersell the historiographical dimensions of Haynes's films, in which allegory emerges from a well-crafted, indeed naturalistic, replication of the past. "Put simply," writes Jonathan Kahana, "allegory is a story that explains one thing by being a story about something else."[28] In Haynes's hands, that "something else" is often a lovingly resurrected historical past, complete with material artifacts, like the props of the 1950s that, first used in Sirk's *Written on the Wind*, would be recycled in Haynes's *Far from Heaven*.[29] (That the props were, in their own time, mere simulations of historical reality—synthetic markers of 1950s America, instruments of "movie magic"—does not deprive them of their status as historical objects; they coexist, in *Far from Heaven*, with vintage products from the CorningWare and Pyrex lines as well as with an actual NAACP brochure

borrowed from the organization's archives.) Haynes hides the
present in the past as a condition of his allegorical operations,
and such concealment depends on a believable rendering of
history—on "the past recaptured." Haynes's period reconstruc-
tions—"affective vision[s] of the past"—are the products of his
close collaborations with various art directors and set decora-
tors, among many others.[30] "I am indebted," Haynes concludes
his introduction to a book containing three of his screenplays,
"to a vast assortment of extraordinary artists and collaborators
without whom these experiments in shape and feeling would
surely have failed."[31]

   I'm Not There is, in Haynes's words, "a set of stories derived
from Dylan's life and mythmaking," and each story has "a very
specific place, setting, moment, history."[32] That is perhaps why
Haynes chose to leave out the 1980s—not because the decade
marked, for Dylan, "an awkward period of overproduction
and strained vocals" but because it was "the beginning of an
era (which, like his tour, never ended) in which Dylan consciously avoided keeping up with the times [and] simply created his own."[33] Haynes, for all his audacity, is not known for
fashioning his own epochs but for plumbing the past—even,
as *Dark Waters* indicates, the recent past—for its emotional
and intellectual potency. In *Velvet Goldmine*, he offers a particularly scathing depiction of the commercial opportunism
of the eighties phase of David Bowie's career. The liberating,
anti-identitarian era of glam rock having ended, Brian Slade
simply and cannily transforms himself into the slick, conservative Tommy Stone, who shamelessly says of "President
Reynolds" (Haynes's stand-in for Ronald Reagan), "I think
he's doing brilliant work. He's a tremendous leader, a tremendous spokesperson for the needs of the nation today." (Stone is

clearly, and probably consciously, echoing the subway ads visible in an earlier shot: "PRESIDENT REYNOLDS REDEEMS AMERICA," they read.) Bowie's commercially triumphant Serious Moonlight Tour becomes, in *Velvet Goldmine*, a concert series promoting Stone's blandly titled album *People Rocking People*. The president's Committee for Cultural Renewal sponsors a television broadcast of one of Stone's concerts. This, Haynes has made clear, is his reproving take on what he terms "the Thatcherized Bowie."[34]

But it is precisely the kind of critique that he does *not* extend to Dylan in *I'm Not There*. Perhaps, then, omitting the eighties was a gesture of restraint—a way of avoiding the dismal fact that, for Dylan, the decade represented a low point, both creatively and commercially. The eighties may have been dark indeed for longtime Bowie fans hoping in vain for a more oppositional display from their beloved star. For Dylan, though, they were darker in a different way—years during which his career as a solo artist seemed on the verge of total collapse. Dylan's own take on his eighties self is certainly uncharitable: the windows of his mind were "boarded up" and "covered with cobwebs," he writes in *Chronicles*; he was "wasted out professionally" and "in the bottomless pit of cultural oblivion."[35] (One need only watch the horrifying *Hearts of Fire* to understand what he means.) Haynes's rather merciful omission of this period raises questions about the kind of gratitude (bordering on obsequiousness) that full cooperation can, if not demand, then at least encourage. David Yaffe writes, "Haynes was given the keys to the kingdom." Here was "one artist allowed to tap into the unconscious of another." "Access often spells limits," Yaffe continues, "but for Haynes, access allowed him to take as weird a trip as he wanted."[36] This isn't necessarily true. The elision of the eighties suggests, perhaps, a certain self-censorship—a normative restraint born of indebtedness to an unexpectedly generous party. It also, conceivably, indicates an attempt at commercial self-protection. After all, the partly mournful, occasionally denunciatory *Velvet Goldmine* failed at the box office.

Dylan obviously did Haynes a favor by signing off on *I'm Not There*, and Haynes, in refraining from depicting arguably the least fertile period of Dylan's career, was perhaps returning that favor. Yet such a psychological explanation may distract from the fact that Haynes, working closely with cinematographer Edward Lachman, had always intended to re-create the 1960s, the decade that immediately followed the events (and styles) explored in his previous film, *Far from Heaven*. For *I'm Not There*, Haynes made ample use of old Kodak film stock, explaining that he "even wanted the film to *look* as if it were from the '60s."[37] Rather than following the twenty-first-century trend of shooting in color and then converting the footage into black-and-white during the printing stage, Lachman shot "real black-and-white" using stock that Kodak had not upgraded in decades. "If I shoot [with Kodak's black-and-white negative film] Double-X in 2006," he said, "it's like shooting it back in the sixties [because] they haven't T-grained it [or employed tabular crystals to improve resolution and granularity] the way they have their color stocks."[38] The movie's "period feel" was further generated by the use of vintage Cooke Panchro lenses, which concentrate resolution in the center of the image. For the Billy the Kid section, shot in color, fifty-year-old zoom lenses were employed to recapture the visual grammar of Peckinpah (as well as of Robert Altman's *McCabe & Mrs. Miller* [1971]). Even Club Silver, the London venue to which

Jude Quinn repairs at one point, was shot to evoke a famous Volkswagen print campaign of the early sixties.[39] It is also patterned on *Who Are You, Polly Maggoo?*, the 1966 French film by American expatriate (and former *Vogue* fashion photographer) William Klein, whose influence Haynes has acknowledged.[40] A parody of documentary portraiture, *Polly Maggoo* depicts the production of an episode of the (fictional) French television series *Who Are You?* Centered on an American fashion model— the Polly of the film's title (played by Dorothy McGowan)—the episode is an attempt to "find the truth beneath the makeup," as its producers so naïvely put it. Shot in black-and-white, Klein's film offers an outré account of Parisian haute couture that anticipates the psychedelia of Haynes's Club Silver even as it recalls *Citizen Kane*. But *Polly Maggoo* also shares broader concerns with *I'm Not There*. The hotly pursued title character, appearing before the handheld cameras of state-run OK-TV, says, "Who am I? I'm Polly Maggoo. But just between us, I'm not sure how to answer. You want to know who I am? I sometimes wonder myself." Jean Rochefort's Grégoire, one of the producers of the *actualité* television program, is convinced that Polly's persona is but a "masquerade": "What's behind the mask? Nothing—or just another mask, and another." Still, he stalks Polly amid the clutter and chaos of her life. (Like Jude Quinn, she collects magazines and clippings; the walls of her Paris apartment comprise a four-paneled collage.) In *I'm Not There*, Bruce Greenwood's Keenan Jones, a journalist for the BBC, trails Quinn in a similar fashion and to equivalent ends, his quest—for the core meaning of an enigma—a commentary on the quintessential generational clash of the 1960s.

None of this is to deny that there are scenes in *I'm Not There* that appear to take place, if not "outside of time," then in some

Keenan Jones confronts the mighty Quinn.

indeterminate amalgam of historical periods. (The film was
even finished using the digital-intermediate process, which,
to facilitate color correction and other last-minute duties, imposed a certain uniformity—still relatively new in 2007—on
the various image formats; in addition to vintage black-and-
white, the latter included the latest color stocks.)[41] The township of Riddle, in particular, seems imprecisely situated, not
geographically (a sign at a train stop identifies its location as
Missouri, for which the Canadian province of Quebec had to
stand in for the filmmakers) but temporally. Missouri became
a state in 1821, and many of the sartorial choices on display
among the residents of Riddle seem to postdate that year by
at least four decades. (Consider, for instance, the Lincoln on
stilts.) Yet it is impossible to say when, exactly, the Riddle
scenes are set; they evoke the odd atemporality of *Masked
and Anonymous*, in which John Goodman's hearty impresa-
rio, introducing a collection of carny characters (including a
Lincoln impersonator), calls it "the greatest human menag-
erie since the Stone Age" (since Chaplin set sail?). Throughout
I'm Not There, Haynes references Dylan's famous defiance of

chronology—a motif perhaps most memorably employed in "My Back Pages" (1964), marked by the refrain "Ah, but I was so much older then / I'm younger than that now." "My current situation far precedes anything from the past," Coco Rivington tells Jude Quinn, expressing precisely the sort of inconsecutiveness that Haynes's nonlinear narrative enacts. As Gere's Billy the Kid puts it in voice-over at the close of the film, after finding Guthrie's guitar in a boxcar en route to someplace other than Riddle, "It's like you got yesterday, today, and tomorrow all in the same room. There's no telling what can happen."

VISIONS OF VIETNAM

Images of the Vietnam War seem to intrude on Billy the Kid, as they do on the characters in *Petulia*. The verdant hills of Riddle suggest the lush vegetation of Southeast Asia, and Haynes is soon juxtaposing the two environments, offering brief, near-subliminal flashes of the latter as Billy, on horseback, contemplates the former. Shots of his stricken face suggest that he, too, can see these visions of Vietnam—that he has ocular as well as emotional access to this different place (and, perhaps, to a different time—the future?). At a later moment, having taken a long, last look behind him, Billy rides his horse away from the camera. He is ostensibly pursuing his dog, the hound having bolted toward the township of Riddle as though magnetized by something there. Billy, too, seems entranced. As he rides, Robbie's gentle voice-over begins its wry synopsis of the events of 1968. The latter's words mix with the fading strains of Dylan's "One More Cup of Coffee," as well as with the hoofbeats of Billy's departing steed. "1968," begins Robbie's sound bridge. "America watched its war plan collapse, its cities

Alone together.

burn, its youth erupt, its president crumble, its greatest leaders fall slain. And there we were—all alone with Richard Nixon." (In *Chronicles*, Dylan offers a similarly apocalyptic summary of 1968, writing, "America was wrapped up in a blanket of rage. Students at universities were wrecking parked cars, smashing windows. The war in Vietnam was sending the country into a deep depression. The cities were in flames, the bludgeons were coming down.")[42] A medium close-up of Claire shows her sitting stock-still and staring off into the distance, her face bathed in the bluish light of dusk. Suddenly—a photograph come to life, as in Chris Marker's *La Jetée* (1962)—she looks down, and the camera, panning in pursuit of the object of her gaze, reveals that she is holding an infant, in a pose that suggests the Madonna and Child, particularly as painted by Raphael.

Robbie, seated next to Claire and talking politics with another couple, mentions the Bible only moments later. Placed at a table on a restaurant's back patio, berating his liberal friends for their reputedly naïve beliefs, Robbie stakes his claim to a kind of nihilism that he tries to pass off as sophistication. As early as 1968—that annus mirabilis of global protest—he is

saying, "Face it: it's over." Nixon's election to the presidency
appears to have sealed his sense of apocalypse. ("What's with
all this doomsday hocus-pocus going around?" Billy asks the
residents of Riddle; failing to receive a convincing answer, he
finally concedes "the thrill of waiting up for the end of the
world.") "All these groups promoting the movement are so full
of their own . . . bullshit," Robbie continues. Then, accusing his
tablemates of being simpleminded, he adds, "You just think
it's all about *them*, man—all these right-wing corporate hawks
plotting to invade the world and drug us to death with happy
pills and the Bible." He is beginning to sound like the character he played in *Grain of Sand*, with his sweeping complaints
and childlike whine ("It's not about *me* anymore—it's all about
him."). Earlier in the film, Greenwood's journalist asks Jude
Quinn for clarification: "Would you say, then, that the collective struggles of the color discrimination or the war have
failed, or . . . do you think it's the process itself that's at fault?"
Patently impatient with this line of questioning, Jude replies,
"Who cares what I think? I'm not the president." Johnson is
in office when Jude speaks these words, while Nixon is Robbie's presidential referent, a figure whose all-too-obvious faults
seem to inspire, or simply exacerbate, Robbie's near-existen-
tial despair (which he yet expresses smugly, with a shit-eating
grin on his matinee-idol face). Robbie's friend, suddenly in
the position of a celebrity at a press conference, hounded to
account for his past utterances, gives a Dylanesque answer:
"I never said that." Robbie, reduced now to the literal-mind-
edness of journalistic inquiry (at least as he and two of the
film's other Dylans so brusquely understand it, from their lofty
positions as perpetual interviewees), replies, "What are you
talking about? You say it all the time." Robbie, who insists

that "it's over" (without once defining what "it" is), seems obsessed with the sense of an ending that he repeatedly attempts to impose. ("I'm not part of no Movement," Dylan told Nat Hentoff in 1964. "If I was, I wouldn't be able to do anything else but be in 'the Movement.' I just can't make it with any organization.")[43] "That's when she knew it was over for good," Robbie says in voice-over, as Claire, in an earlier scene, catches Nixon addressing the nation and announcing an agreement on "ending the war and restoring peace" in Vietnam. "The longest-running war in television history, the war that hung like a shadow over the same nine years of her marriage. So why was it suddenly so hard to breathe?" Possibly, as Haynes may well have understood, because the war in fact lasted far longer than nine years.

Haynes embraces, and perhaps critiques, the cliché of Vietnam as a "television war." In *No Direction Home*, Scorsese includes portions of Morley Safer's CBS News coverage of the burning of Cam Ne—critical coverage that, of course, represented but one point on the dial. (When, in *Factory Girl*, Andy Warhol and Edie Sedgwick are asked to give an opinion on the war, the latter replies, "We prefer *I Dream of Jeannie*.") Television sets and feeds form a frequent presence in *I'm Not There*, as in all of Haynes's previous films. (In *Safe*, it is a hospital TV that informs Carol White about "environmental illness," giving her possible insight into her mysterious condition—or, perhaps, "creating" that condition by bringing it further into discourse.) Defending Dylan against charges that he was blissfully unaware of the Vietnam War (or "that whole Nam business," as a Columbia Records executive puts it in the program on Jack Rollins), David Yaffe writes, "He had a television; he knew what was going on."[44] Televised images of racial strife

at home and imperialist violence abroad appear to have infil-
trated Jude Quinn's dreams, even as he refuses, in his waking
life, to directly acknowledge their impact. An overhead shot
of the star passed out on the floor of some hotel room is interrupted by a rapid-fire montage that, consisting of frames from
various documentary records of assassinations and bombings,
recalls the "montage test" in Alan J. Pakula's 1974 thriller *The
Parallax View* (a favorite of Haynes), as well as a similar succession of images that punctuates *Superstar* ("The year is 1970
. . .").[45] Reviewing *I'm Not There* in the *New Yorker*, Anthony
Lane complained of Haynes's montage, "Why palm off on us a
few stock-footage shots of Martin Luther King Jr., mass riots,
and Nixon's declaring an end to the war in Vietnam? How can
we judge Dylan's place in history, when the history feels paper
thin?"[46] This objection to Haynes's use of "history" perhaps
misses the point (as does Lane's similarly obtuse criticism of
the Bale/Rollins section for evoking Christopher Guest's 2003
mockumentary *A Mighty Wind*): the mediation of public life
can only ever "feel paper thin"; endlessly repeated, all images
come to seem like "stock-footage shots," whatever their purpose or provenance. But they are also, to quote Sean Latham's
description of Dylan's creative process, "scaffolds on which new
and familiar ideas can be arranged."[47]

Haynes directly represents this phenomenon through
Jude's obsessive collection of newspaper and magazine clippings; shots of such assiduous collaging suggest not simply
the cover of Dylan's 1965 album *Bringing It All Back Home*,
which shows Dylan seated amid a pile of mass-circulation publications (including an issue of *Time* that proclaims President
Johnson "Man of the Year"), but also the amalgamating techniques that Haynes and Dylan share. Haynes's aim is not to

pursue the anthropological practice of thick description, with its connotations of public intellectualism and holistic understanding, but to indicate the thinness of history as distilled through representational media. That the "stock-footage shots" are hyperfamiliar is part of the point: Haynes is drawing on an archive that we think we know. But he also seems to be questioning the very concept of familiarity, as if to suggest not simply that meanings change over time but also that they were never stable, never fixed or explicable, to begin with. ("What does it mean?" asks a little boy in *Wonderstruck*, pointing to a line by Oscar Wilde; his mother replies with a question of her own: "Well, what do you *think* it means?") In 1975, "Rolling Thunder" might have been known to many as the name of the massive air war that the United States had begun in Southeast Asia some ten years earlier, and that had come to include the bombing of more than just military targets. (Devastating North Vietnam, the aerial bombardments also spilled over into Cambodia and Laos.) But was Dylan, in adopting the operation's name in the wake of the US military defeat, embracing or critiquing the country's aerial wrath? The national itinerary of the Rolling Thunder Revue, which included stops at war memorials in Rochester and New Haven, even evoked Operation Rolling Thunder's expansive, ecumenical target list, which President Johnson handpicked at his Tuesday lunches.[48] By placing Dylan's words in President Johnson's mouth, Haynes suggests a murderous affinity between the two men ("Death to all those who would whimper and cry"). For her part, Joan Baez vigorously opposed the Johnson administration's military policies, and she happened to be in Hanoi during a horrific aerial bombing campaign in December 1972.[49] Haynes includes archival footage of such strategic bombing in both

Superstar and *I'm Not There*. If this momentous history "feels paper-thin," it may only be to a certain kind of viewer.

References to Vietnam abound in *Masked and Anonymous*. Even the infamous My Lai massacre is evoked through Giovanni Ribisi's tearful monologue, in which his character confesses to having participated in the slaughter of women and children in a remote village. Expressing no allegiances, willing to fight on any side, he soon found himself killing noncombatants under government orders, as he tells Dylan's sphinxlike Jack Fate. In *I'm Not There*, Robbie Clark also suggests the dangers of noninvolvement—the politically calamitous consequences of an "apolitical" stance. During preproduction, Haynes wrote in his notebook that the relationship between Robbie and Claire was to be "doomed to a long stubborn protraction (not unlike Vietnam, which it parallels)."[50] Yet this is perhaps too pat a mapping of the personal onto the political, of the domestic onto the world-historical—not least of all in the suggestion that a sort of rebirth or renewal (of Claire, of America) will follow the cessation of hostilities. Claire breaks free of a bad marriage; the United States extricates itself from the "quagmire" in Southeast Asia. But Haynes also indicates that, ultimately, disentanglement may not be possible: Claire is last seen magnetized by the televised image of Robbie in *Grain of Sand*, and the United States, like Dylan, is spared the representation of any post-1980 development.

EVERYBODY MUST GET SUED

Like Dylan himself, *I'm Not There* challenges conventional conceptions of authorship—unless, that is, the film can be said to confirm equally familiar ideas about folk culture as collectively constituted, endlessly reiterative, and fundamentally nonproprietary. The irony is that Dylan, who has disavowed his connection to folk art at least as often as he has strategically embraced it, is both a well-protected owner of intellectual property and a not-infrequent target of copyright complaints. (As David Yaffe puts it, pointing to the transformative factor of contract law, "When Dylan was learning songs from fellow musicians on Bleecker Street, everything was shared. All that changed when he signed his name on the dotted line. Originality became not only a creative or philosophical matter but [also] a legal one. Recording contracts made all the difference, and they changed all the expectations.")[51] When the songwriter James Damiano sued Dylan and Sony Music Entertainment in 1996, he claimed that Dylan had used portions of six of his works without permission. The case, which was heard in a federal court in New Jersey, where Damiano's complaint was originally filed, hinged on competing interpretations of the "threshold of originality"—a key concept in copyright law. Damiano, who was able to demonstrate that Dylan in fact had access to his work, took an extreme position, asking the court to grant him a monopoly over some rather common word combinations (including the joining of "bell" and "hell"), while the defendants maintained that Dylan's use of clichéd phrases (like "buried deep down inside" and "free your body") were simply not copyrightable—not even by Dylan. The court found in favor of the latter. Damiano, it turned out, had merely sought to create the impression of plagiarism by "cherry-picking" elements of his own compositions, pasting them together, and placing them alongside incomplete and otherwise altered transcriptions of Dylan's lyrics. Even on its own, profoundly misleading terms, however, the plaintiff's carefully collaged approximation of artistic theft was deemed meritless, as the words in question were insufficiently "original." (One could, of course, argue that Damiano, with his propensity for collage, simply did what Dylan does; deriding his "cut-and-paste" approach, the court described what, in the hands of a Dylan or a Todd Haynes, is almost reflexively celebrated as pastiche.) The court, furthermore, expressed concern not necessarily for Dylan (though his lawyers had asserted that the plaintiff's complaint was frivolous, and they had sought dismissal as a sanction) but rather for any artist whose creativity might be stifled by an unwarranted fear of plagiarism—precisely the sort of fear that complaints like Damiano's threatened to engender.[52]

Yet Dylan has been similarly litigious. If his complaints have occasionally seemed just as groundless as Damiano's, his corporate backing, legal muscle, and sheer star power have often been sufficient to frighten and subdue potential defendants. Shortly before the scheduled release of the Weinstein Company's Edie Sedgwick biopic *Factory Girl* in the fall of 2006, Dylan issued a legal action against the filmmakers, demanding the immediate cancellation of all theatrical bookings. The film's production had already been a rocky one, with last-minute reshoots intended, in part, to preclude the sort of punitive action that Dylan would eventually pursue.[53] Originally cast as Dylan, actor Hayden Christensen proceeded to play the role in blatant imitation of the star even after the character's name was changed, first to "Billy Quinn" ("Quinn" being closely associated with Dylan, who composed and recorded the folk-rock song "Quinn the Eskimo," also known as "The Mighty Quinn," in 1967, during the *Basement Tapes* sessions), and finally to the ostentatiously nonspecific "Musician" (the name that would ultimately appear in the film's closing credits). George Hickenlooper, the director of *Factory Girl*, later claimed that the problems had begun long before Dylan threatened to take legal action: in order for the production to receive insurance, Dylan's name had to be scrubbed from the script. Yet Christensen, famous for his appearances in the *Star Wars* franchise, was crucial to the financing, and he insisted on retaining the Dylan impersonation that he had so carefully devised. Hickenlooper, beholden to Christensen's star power, did not attempt to dissuade the actor. The result, variously described (at least by those looking to counter charges of defamation) as "this sixties version of Bono" and some amalgamation of Dylan, Donovan, Mick Jagger, and Jim Morrison, is clearly and exclusively Dylan (though no false nose is used; as in *I'm Not There*, hair, voice, and costume bear much of the burden of suggesting the embodied artist, whose famously prominent nose is almost never matched, whether naturally or through prosthetics, by the performers who portray him in popular media).[54] "I was never trying to say that Hayden Christensen was not Bob Dylan," Hickenlooper told *New York* magazine in February 2007, some two months after Dylan first instructed his legal team to go after the Weinstein Company. "It was the lawyers who were telling me to shut up."[55]

If Hickenlooper was confident ("Bob Dylan is not going to sue us," he said), the Weinstein Company was possibly less so.[56] Though Dylan had not yet seen *Factory Girl*, his lawyer, Orin Snyder, claimed of the film's original screenplay (by Captain Mauzner, who had cowritten the 2003 John Holmes biopic *Wonderland*) that it clearly suggested Dylan was morally culpable for Edie Sedgwick's "tragic decline into heroin addiction and eventual suicide." *Factory Girl* represented the resurfacing, and embellishment, of long-simmering rumors regarding Dylan's relationship with Sedgwick (which, whatever its exact nature, is often said to have inspired such caustic "kiss-off" songs as "Just Like a Woman" and "Like a Rolling Stone"). "You appear," Snyder wrote to the Weinstein Company, "to be laboring under the misunderstanding that merely changing the name of a character or making him a purported fictional composite will immunize you from suit. That is not so. Even though Mr. Dylan's name is not used, the portrayal remains both defamatory and a violation of Mr. Dylan's right of publicity."[57]

In an early scene, set in 1959, *I'm Not There* offers an amusing meditation on the concept of the "fictional composite": Marcus Carl Franklin's Woody Guthrie, the first version of Dylan to receive substantial screen time (and one of three bearing the names of actual historical subjects—Ben Whishaw's Arthur Rimbaud and Richard Gere's Billy the Kid are the others), is asked if there is "really a town called Riddle" (the place from which Guthrie claims to hail). In response, Guthrie says, "To tell you the flat truth, that's sort of a . . . a whatchamacallit." "A composite," suggests his interlocutor, to which Guthrie cheerfully replies, "A compost heap is more like it!" Except for a couple of minor alterations (the addition of a single determiner here, the removal of another there), the exchange is taken verbatim from Kazan's *A Face in the Crowd*. As the historian Sean Wilentz points out in his book *Bob Dylan in America*, "Dylan saw *A Face in the Crowd* in the Village in 1962 and, reportedly, was more shaken by it than by any film he'd seen since *Rebel Without a Cause* or *The Wild One*." Wilentz draws attention to the function in Kazan's film of the folk song "The Roving Gambler," which turns "exuberant and menacing" in Lonesome Rhodes's megalomaniacal hands.[58] (It is in this sense that *A Face in the Crowd* most powerfully anticipates Tim Robbins's 1992 satire *Bob Roberts*, in which the title figure, a deeply conservative senatorial candidate, communicates his right-wing views through folk songs, placing genocidal sentiments in a deceptively gentle idiom.) "A compost heap is more like it!" is also the kind of memorable movie line that someone—a kid, say—might steal in 1959, just two years after the release of *A Face in the Crowd*. It makes sense that the eleven-year-old Woody uses it, though such plausibility is, perhaps, of secondary importance—incidental to Haynes's allusiveness, which rarely, if ever, requires a psychological pretext.

By having Franklin's Guthrie speak the words of Andy Griffith's Lonesome Rhodes—the "grassroots fascist" of *A Face in the Crowd*—Haynes complicates any easy correspondence between politics and art. ("It's lonesome roads we shall walk," Woody says at one point.) Announcing its own antifascist power, Guthrie's guitar suggests the ultimate emptiness of sloganeering. For the instrument cannot, on its own, guarantee that a politically progressive message will be received—or even performed. Guthrie, as played by a child actor, is indisputably unformed, whatever his bluster. He may well face the very temptations that transform Lonesome Rhodes from one kind of populist—"homespun" and altogether benign—into another. Indeed, *A Face in the Crowd* suggests the danger of political investment in celebrity—of using *any* star persona, even one as seemingly stable and progressive as Rhodes's initially appears, as one's political compass. For the mutable Rhodes quickly, and perhaps inevitably, becomes a mouthpiece for staunch conservatism as well as a richly rewarded instrument of the elite. Consider the ease with which he improvises, live on the air, a lament for the loss of Britain's overseas colonies—a bitter jeremiad that seamlessly morphs into a statement of American superiority, and an implicit call to requisition the forfeited lands of the older empire.

The riskiness of reading progressivism into celebrity—*any* kind of celebrity—is central to *I'm Not There*. Underscoring Guthrie's dishonesty, the reference to Rhodes also prepares for the film's depiction of the disappointment of audiences forced to confront Jude Quinn's unexpected pivot away from protest songs, which seems to accompany his sudden "electrification" at the 1965 Newport Folk Festival (or, as it is renamed here, the "New England Jazz & Folk Festival"). This, too, is experienced as a political betrayal, much to Quinn's chagrin. Later, as in *A Face in the Crowd*, the medium of television, however debased or maligned, emerges as a transmission belt for "truth." It retains its revelatory capacity, which, under constant threat of suppression, requires the deliberate intervention of others— whether that of Patricia Neal's conscience-stricken producer, who, at the climax of the Kazan film, disrupts technical norms in order to expose the "real" Lonesome Rhodes, or of Quinn's active viewer, who must turn the dial in order to ward off the mind-numbing monotony of a Western program. (Characters are constantly changing channels in *I'm Not There*, which features more television sets than any other Haynes film.) In *Chronicles*, Dylan recalls turning on a black-and-white TV in the Village in the early 1960s and finding a Western series so self-consciously "American" that it appeared to come from another land: "*Wagon Train* was on. It seemed to be beaming in from some foreign country."[59] By passing over just such a program and seeking out a public-affairs series called *Culture Beat*, Quinn models a form of television spectatorship conceivably open to the manipulable mass audience in *A Face in the Crowd*: changing the channel is, after all, always an option (though the BBC, on which *Culture Beat* is broadcast, is certainly a rarefied example, ostensibly far removed from the American context of commercial television). So, of course, is tuning out. As Michael DeAngelis observes, the medium can be "piercing"; it offers an "impact [that] Jude manages to diffuse only by shutting off the television set."[60]

Keenan Jones, the suave host of *Culture Beat*, takes to the airwaves to "expose" Jude Quinn. Directly addressing the camera, he lays out the previously occluded biographical facts, first noting that "for so many of his ardent admirers, Quinn's simple raggedness was always the sign of his truth. In it they could always conjure all the hard knocks his rough-and-tumble story implies—the honest struggles their far more conventional backgrounds deny them." "Quinn's recent foray into electronic music has raised doubts concerning his sincerity in the past," Jones continues. Sharing his "scoop" with evident relish, the reporter (who here recalls Alistair Cooke's stint as homiletic host of *Omnibus*) describes "the real Jude Quinn" as "suburban, middle class, educated, [and] as conventional as they come— the eldest son of a Brookline, Massachusetts, department-store owner. The real name of America's backwoods-vagabond-turned-rock-and-roll-martyr is *Aaron Jacob Edelstein*." The pleasure that Jones derives from this unveiling verges on the sadistic. More than mere reportage is transpiring here: Jones's punitive tone becomes downright murderous when he predicts that "the startling truth behind [Jude's] famously clouded origins is sure to close the book, once and for all, on his future." Broadcast television, even in the middlebrow form of the BBC's *Culture Beat*, is an assassin.

Jones's televised triumph.

That Dylan was, in fact, something other than a rootless troubadour was first communicated to a mass public via an article in the November 4, 1963, issue of *Newsweek*. "His audiences share his pain, and seem jealous because they grew up in conventional homes and conventional schools," the article asserted. "The ironic thing is that Bob Dylan, too, grew up in a conventional home, and went to conventional schools. He shrouds his past in contradictions, but he is the elder son of a Hibbing, Minnesota, appliance dealer named Abe Zimmerman, and, as Bobby Zimmerman, he attended Hibbing High School, then briefly the University of Minnesota."[61] It is instructive that Haynes changes the medium of Dylan's unmasking even as he extensively quotes the *Newsweek* article, placing its words in the mouth of television's Mr. Jones. An inherited suspicion of broadcast media seeps into Haynes's portrayal of the reporter, who functions as Jude's tormenter, stalking the star in a manner that suggests Nabokov's Clare Quilty (particularly as portrayed by Peter Sellers in Stanley Kubrick's 1962 film of *Lolita*). Like the Quilty who so perversely mirrors protagonist Humbert Humbert, Jones shares a certain mass-media celebrity with Jude. (In *Masked and Anonymous*, Jeff Bridges's relentless reporter, who hounds Dylan's Jack Fate, badgering the rock star with all manner of "personal" questions, is also the other man's double, at least sartorially.) Both are public figures: Jude has a stage, Jones his own TV show. The reporter's retinue seems even larger than that of the rock star. At its apex is an uppity assistant who scolds Jude's manager, warning him that Jones has "no time at all" and "seldom does interviews." "He's really much more of an opinion maker, really, on the telly," she adds. Later, Jones is likened to the movie star Victor Mature (while Jude, ever puckish, registers his resemblance to Elsa Lanchester). Though the rock star fancies himself a disobliging subject ("No, I shall not cooperate with reporters' whims," Dylan pledged in 1963),[62] Jude gives Jones exactly what the latter wants: the sort of wordy indirection that bespeaks a guilty conscience. Jude is, clearly, someone with something to hide—something that Jones can "uncover" on the air. The reporter's ambition is as pronounced as Jude's own—and just as frequently disavowed.

Itself a fictionalized account of Dylan's career, *Hearts of Fire* shares with *I'm Not There* a certain interest in television's capacity to get under a celebrity's otherwise well-protected skin—to penetrate the conscience of a recalcitrant public figure. Ensconced in his London hotel room, Dylan's character watches a documentary television program that describes him in unflattering terms. The scene closely mirrors its counterpart in Haynes's film, up until the point at which Dylan's enraged rock star, acting out a familiar bad-boy persona, picks up the television set and tosses it through a window; he proceeds to trash the rest of the room, so offended is he by the program's succinct critique of his carefully cultivated persona. Yet

Hearts of Fire is not interested in the methods or motivations of mass-media personalities. Haynes, by contrast, has Jones bribing people (including Jude's manager) for "scoops," placing large wads of cash in their hands in what may or may not be "just" a dream sequence or an imagined music video. Jones clearly has a capacity for corruption.

STUCK INSIDE OF GALLUP

By quoting Kazan's *A Face in the Crowd*, *I'm Not There* evokes Dylan's own tendency to misdirect. One conspicuous example, included in *No Direction Home*, is Dylan's early interview with Oscar Brand of WNYC Radio, during which Brand asked Dylan where he was raised and the latter replied with the name of a place—Gallup, New Mexico—that he had, in fact, never even visited. There really is a Riddle, Oregon, just as there really is a Gallup, New Mexico, though the Riddle depicted in *I'm Not There* is meant to be in Missouri—a sign indicates as much when Gere's Billy the Kid, late in the film, flees the township by train.

The Brand interview—Dylan's radio debut—was conducted just a few years after the release of *A Face in the Crowd*, and it had its own filmic reverberations. In mentioning Gallup, Dylan named not only a quintessentially "Western" city but also one with a privileged relationship to Hollywood cinema. The list of films shot on location in Gallup is long, and it includes several titles that the ever-shifting Dylan persona would cite in some way and that *I'm Not There* would, in its own turn, reflect: King Vidor's *Billy the Kid* (1930), filmed by MGM in an early widescreen process called Realife, using 70-millimeter Grandeur cameras rented from the Fox Film Corporation, was among the prototypes of the Peckinpah Western in which Dylan would appear; John Ford's *The Grapes of Wrath* (1940), the famous adaptation of the Steinbeck novel (a favorite of high-school student Robert Allen Zimmerman, who penned a twenty-two-page paper on it for an English class)[63] about tenant farmers fleeing the Dust Bowl, exerted an obvious influence on Dylan's "folk" period; and *Pursued* (1947), a noir Western—arguably the very first such hybrid—that is perhaps most "Dylanesque" in its attention to family origins that are forgotten or suppressed, to be replaced by an indeterminate and entirely self-sustaining persona.

Two other films shot on location in Gallup bear mentioning for their connections to Dylan's persona and career. Taken together, and read in relation to Dylan's ever-challenging creative output, they help illuminate some of the less palatable components of Haynes's portrait of the artist. William Keighley's *Rocky Mountain* (1950) and John Sturges's *Escape from Fort Bravo* (1953), major Hollywood productions about the Civil War, both offer distinctly sympathetic portrayals of Confederate soldiers, and both use Gallup—Dylan's Gallup, that emblem of the West—as the setting for rapprochements between blue and gray. In each instance, an "Indian attack" precipitates the détente. In *Rocky Mountain*, Shoshone warriors compel a Confederate patrol (led by Errol Flynn's Mississippi-born captain) to collaborate with Union troops. By the end of the film, all of the Southerners are dead—victims of the "red man's" aggression. To honor the rebels' courage, a Union army officer raises the Confederate battle flag atop the Rockies, and it is with this rather startling image—a low-angle shot of the symbol of white supremacy, bathed in sunlight and flapping in the wind—that the film ends. (Seconds before the final fade-out, scores of Northerners and a dog salute the rebel flag—the canine by closing his eyes in apparent satisfaction—as a heavenly chorus sings a slow, sorrowful version of "Dixie," transforming the typically jaunty song into a dirge, much in the manner of Dylan's later transmutations of traditional music; Dylan even performs "Dixie" in *Masked and Anonymous*.) The film's opening is perhaps equally provocative: a modern automobile—a 1950 Chevrolet Deluxe—drives through Gallup, stopping at a (fake) historical marker commemorating the fictional saga that the film will dramatize in flashback. (The rather wordy plaque ends with its own tribute to the Confederates: "Though their mission failed, the heroism displayed by these gallant men honored the cause for which they fought so valiantly.") The Anscocolor *Escape from Fort Bravo*, starring William Holden and Eleanor Parker, is perhaps less audacious, but it similarly redeems its Confederate characters, including a young soldier who, through his encounter with "fierce" Mescalero Apaches, proves that he is not a coward.

In mining the past, Dylan does not appear to make any moral distinctions. Sean Wilentz has written that the superstar "took inspiration from the gray as well as the blue."[64] So, of course, did the classical Hollywood cinema—an approach that is all but unthinkable today. It is worth emphasizing the centrality of the Lost Cause mythology to both *Rocky Mountain* and *Escape from Fort Bravo* because Dylan, whose interest in the 1860s is well known (he describes himself as a Civil War buff in *Chronicles*), was accused of helping to promulgate that mythology through his involvement in Ronald F. Maxwell's controversial war film *Gods and Generals* (2003). Personally financed by Atlanta-based billionaire Ted Turner,

Gods and Generals echoes the earlier Westerns in its flattering portrayal of the Confederacy. It also features Dylan's original song "'Cross the Green Mountain," commissioned specifically for the film and written to suit its nostalgic spirit. Dylan even stars (as a kind of Civil War "type," flintlock pistol and all) in the associated music video, which evokes the laments for the Confederate dead with which both *Rocky Mountain* and *Escape from Fort Bravo* end. Dylan's dandyish character (dressed not unlike Whishaw's Rimbaud) passes through a rebel encampment, presides over an impromptu funeral service for a fallen soldier (described as his "merciful friend," in a moment that mirrors, and is intercut with, the mourning of a slain graycoat in *Gods and Generals*), and finally places an ornately framed daguerreotype at the grave of a Virginia cavalryman. (That it is an actual grave—that of Captain W. R. Jeter of the 13th Virginia Cavalry Regiment—grounds Dylan's flourish in the material realities of Confederate genuflection, making clear the physical availability of epitaph-decorated monuments to the Lost Cause.) Wilentz defends the music video as "evenhanded" because it happens to feature, albeit fleetingly, the occasional Union soldier and thus can be said to "depict[] the suffering and boredom of war on both sides." But, as Wilentz concedes, the feature film in whose service the video was made has "a decidedly pro-southern tilt."[65] In fact, both film and music video disproportionately feature, and lavishly lament, Confederate suffering, in the tradition of the Hollywood fictions shot in Gallup. Dylan's lyrics even speak of the spilling of "brave blood." "The world is gray," he sings. "Stars fell over Alabama."

Not surprisingly, conservative groups expressed considerable support for *Gods and Generals*, which was a favorite of

Goin' to Antietam?

Phyllis Schlafly, who praised it for presenting "truthful history" and for avoiding "politically-correct revisionism."[66] After submitting his theme song, Dylan was accused of lifting lines from the poet Henry Timrod, but plagiarism was hardly the only issue at hand, for Timrod is known as the poet laureate of the Confederacy.[67] A South Carolina native whose work helped boost enlistment in the secessionist cause, he published numerous calls to arms. Dylan borrowed from his poetry in both "'Cross the Green Mountain" and his 2006 album *Modern Times*—a pilfering that seemed, to many, doubly indefensible, given Timrod's political allegiances.[68]

When Gregory Peck paid tribute to Dylan at the 1997 Kennedy Center Honors, he began by recalling the sight of Civil War veterans marching in the Independence Day parades of his childhood in La Jolla, California. "The first time I heard Bob Dylan, it brought back that memory," Peck said. "I thought of him as something of a Civil War type—a kind of nineteenth-century troubadour, a maverick American spirit." Peck was essentially repaying Dylan, who, with cowriter Sam Shepard, had cited Peck as an unforgettable screen presence in the song "Brownsville Girl," from Dylan's 1986 album *Knocked Out Loaded*. "The reediness of his voice and the sparseness of his words go straight to the heart of America," Peck added. Yet that heart has long been divided, as during the Civil War, and Dylan's artistic interests have frequently suggested an unseemly fascination with Dixie.

Haynes hardly shies away from this aspect of his subject's career. In her review of *I'm Not There*, critic Kimberly Jones draws attention to the "Civil War getups" worn by many of the residents of Riddle, the township in which Richard Gere's Billy the Kid roams as though in exile.[69] Blackface, too, is part of the landscape here—one performance technique among many. David Yaffe has referred to Dylan—not unreasonably—as "the minstrelsy-obsessed allegorist of the twenty-first century."[70] (Ed Harris briefly appears in blackface in *Masked and Anonymous*, playing the ghost of a famous minstrel.) For Dylan, blackface appears to function less as a definite index of racism and oppression than as an eccentric gesture that resists meaning. In *No Direction Home*, he recalls the circuses of his Minnesota childhood, which featured "George Washington in blackface—stuff that didn't even make any sense." Haynes does not so much defend Dylan's logic as grant it occasional expression. He seems to understand that a certain puckishness is at play here—that Dylan is assuming the role of contrarian in so "naïvely" embracing minstrelsy. "Dylan is a person who is going to challenge orthodoxy, even when it comes out of the left," Haynes has said. Whether questioning "the political correctness of feminism or leftist thought [more generally]," Dylan approaches ideology with considerable skepticism; his impulse, however childish, is to "poke a stick at it."[71] (*No Direction Home* includes a clip of Allen Ginsberg proudly announcing that Dylan is "nobody's left-wing servant.") In a gesture of fidelity to an unsavory aspect of the past—part of the film's apparent re-creation of nineteenth-century America— *I'm Not There* features a white man performing in blackface. Twice glimpsed among the many freaks of Riddle, he gazes toward the camera as if in defiance of the ethical norms of the future.

JOHN DOE REVISITED

The film's shooting script describes the Woody section as "backwoods melodrama, which unfurls from a traveling box-car." In *Chronicles*, Dylan outlines the affective power of rail transport: "I'd seen and heard trains from my earliest child-hood days and the sight and sound of them always made me feel secure. The big boxcars, the iron ore cars, freight cars, passenger trains, Pullman cars."[72] Dylan was born at a time when transportation by train was still practical for many Americans hoping to cover vast distances, but his affection for the boxcar clearly exceeds the vehicle's historical preva-lence to form part of a broader passion for the outmoded, the obsolete. "The madly complicated modern world was some-thing I took little interest in," Dylan claims in *Chronicles*. "It had no relevancy, no weight. I wasn't seduced by it. What was swinging, topical and up to date for me was stuff like the *Ti-tanic* sinking, the Galveston flood, John Henry driving steel, John Hardy shooting a man on the West Virginia line. All this was current, played out and in the open. This was the news that I considered, followed and kept tabs on."[73] Elaborating on Dylan's studied absorption of anachronism, Greil Marcus of-fers an apt description of the eleven-year-old Woody of *I'm Not*

There: "He's a hobo guitar-player in love with the dust-bowl ballads of the Great Depression and trying to live them out."[74] That he's making the attempt in 1959, over two decades after the fact, is clear from the condition of the railway carriages into which he leaps. In sharp contrast to the crowded boxcars of *Bound for Glory*, they are sparsely populated, carrying no more than three occupants at a time—and often just one. The Depression is over; only the occasional dreamer seeks to re-live it during boom times. *Songs for the New Depression*, Bette Midler's third studio album, released in 1976, featured a duet with Bob Dylan. In *I'm Not There*, Dylan's youngest avatar is busy searching for the old slump.

Haynes, too, adopts past styles in putting over the idea of Woody as Depression-obsessed copyist. At one point, the boy, his deceptions threatening to rebound on him, flees in the night. A frontal shot of him walking toward the camera suggests the perilous nature of his nocturnal trek. The eeri-ness is enhanced by the fact that Franklin, the actor portraying Woody, is walking on an unseen treadmill—walking in place, moving without getting anywhere, a bit of trickery that re-calls the studio-bound simulations of an earlier era of movie history, the period with which Woody is plainly preoccupied. A familiar transitional device, this expressionist "summation montage" evokes, specifically, Hollywood films of the thirties and forties. Haynes borrowed it from *Meet John Doe* (1941), Frank Capra's rather muddled account of a hobo who, like Lonesome Rhodes in *A Face in the Crowd*, becomes a national media sensation.[75]

Unlike Rhodes, however, Gary Cooper's John Willoughby is an innocent. Guileless, ingenuous, he places himself in the hands of the striving and the cynical, who manipulate his image—that of the American "Everyman"—for their own ends. Presented to the public as "John Doe"—the quintessential "forgotten man"—Willoughby becomes both symbol and champion of the downtrodden multitudes, who respond to his mass-mediated persona with collective ardor, projecting their own hopes and dreams onto it. More than fifteen thousand "ordinary" Americans eventually assemble for a mass rally—a kind of convention held in support of the "neighborly" ideal that Willoughby, as Doe, represents. Yet it is precisely because Willoughby is every bit as "wholesome" as his press-assigned role that he plans to "come clean" at the convention: he is not a blank slate but a man with a biography; "John Doe" is merely the invention of a newly corporatized newspaper whose powerful publisher has designs on the highest office in the land and hopes to gain the votes of the character's many fans. "The idea is still good," Willoughby feebly maintains of his fiction's underlying premise of hospitality, though it is at risk of being fully captured by an authoritarian personality. The rain-soaked convention becomes the site of a further manipulation when Edward Arnold's newspaper magnate—the man who would be president—preempts Willoughby's attempt to warn the crowd of the threat of a fascist takeover of a "humane" movement. Willoughby tries to explain himself—tries to expose the "frame-up"—but members of the publisher's private police force intervene, cutting the wires that power the loudspeakers, silencing the lone voice of reason. Lusty boos ensue. The previously exalted masses express no skepticism of entrenched power (or even register the technological breakdown). Easily manipulated, they become violent at the slightest provocation.

If Capra's aggrieved conventioneers seem to anticipate Jude Quinn's hostile New England audience, they also, through

Haynes does Vorkapich.

their fearsome displays of violence, force Willoughby to take
refuge in the rural world from whence he has come—a wooded
realm mirrored throughout *I'm Not There*, with its Dylan-
inspired dialectic of city and country, "exposure" and seclusion.
After the mass rally, Willoughby is seen in a pastoral tableau
that evokes Depression-era documentary realism (and thus
many of Dylan's earliest and most familiar referents). Seated
by a creek, flanked by his few belongings (gathered in a bindle)
and a small fire on which to warm some coffee, Willoughby
stares forlornly up at the stars. A nightmarish montage follows, and it is this expressionist vision of persecution—the
work of Slavko Vorkapich, one of Capra's key collaborators,
also responsible for the montages in *Mr. Smith Goes to Washington* (1939)—that Haynes will so assiduously copy in *I'm
Not There*. (For Leland Poague, Vorkapich's contributions to
classical Hollywood suggest nothing less than the "uncertainty
or multiplicity of authorship.")[76] Seen in close-up, a series of
newspaper headlines protest the deception in which Willoughby has participated ("JOHN DOE PROVEN FAKER!"
screams the first). Publication after publication assails him,

even in his dream. (He trudges along, in this darkest of hallucinations, as if "with twenty pounds of headlines stapled to his chest," to quote Dylan's "Stuck Inside of Mobile with the Memphis Blues Again," the first song heard in *I'm Not There*.) Superimposed over the image of Willoughby walking in place is a whirlpool—a privileged image of mental breakdown in forties cinema. Also appearing are the faces of those who shout that he is a "fake" and a "liar" and a "cheat" and an "impostor."

Beyond its reproduction of Willoughby's punishing vision, *I'm Not There* shares several significant devices with *Meet John Doe*. The opening-credit sequences of both films are composed partly of archival footage of laborers and commuters—of "everyday" people at work and at play. Haynes sets his to "Stuck Inside of Mobile with the Memphis Blues Again," while Capra's includes snatches of "Take Me Out to the Ball Game," a 1908 Tin Pan Alley song by Jack Norworth and Albert Von Tilzer, and of two nineteenth-century parlor songs by Stephen Foster ("Hard Times, Come Again No More" and "Oh! Susanna"). Foster, often dubbed the "father of American folk songs" (as in Earl Hobson Smith's 1926 biographical play), was a prolific composer and songwriter, active in the days before recorded music, and Capra uses his works as emblems of Americana.[77] He employs "Take Me Out to the Ball Game" for the same purpose, though Dylan would, in the spoken-word intro to "Bob Dylan's Blues" (1963), famously impugn the province of Tin Pan Alley, contrasting it with his own, exalted location "somewhere down in the United States." Prototypically American in Capra's hands, "Take Me Out to the Ball Game" becomes downright un-American in Dylan's—the synthetic antithesis of his "honest" folk practice.

Capra's film draws extensively on the sort of folk iconography that infuses *I'm Not There*. Richard Gere's Billy the Kid, who will inherit Woody's guitar (and case), powerfully recalls *Meet John Doe*: like Capra's protagonist (and like Woody), he is a frequent rider of boxcars. In both films, as in *Bound for Glory*, such a journey is invariably musical. At one point in *Meet John Doe*, Cooper's Willoughby recalls how he once met a fellow hobo while freight-hopping: the two men bonded over their harmonicas, filling a shared railroad car with melody. To prove their prowess in the present, they play part of Rossini's *William Tell* overture—the theme music for radio's *The Lone Ranger*, which premiered in 1933.

If Gere's Billy the Kid suggests Capra's hobo, he also evokes one of Sam Peckinpah's antisocial protagonists: the title character in the 1970 Western *The Ballad of Cable Hogue*, a desert rat who defends his hermitic existence, contrasting the self-realization of seclusion with a kind of urban anonymity. "In town, I'd be nothing," he says. "I don't like being nothing. . . . Out here, I've got a good start." Eventually, the love of a sympathetic woman—rather than the magnetism of a perversely populated Riddle—draws him out of his isolation. "It's a big world," he concedes. "I wanna see some of it." He makes up his mind to abandon his desert hideaway, first for San Francisco and then for New Orleans. But an emblem of modernity—a horseless carriage, looking eerily anachronistic as it infiltrates Hogue's dusty sanctuary—runs him over. (Fusing *The Ballad of Cable Hogue* and *Pat Garrett and Billy the Kid*, *I'm Not There* has an aged Garrett overseeing efforts to develop Riddle, including by constructing a six-lane interstate highway; the novel automobile is to replace Billy's dependable steed.) As he lies dying, Hogue instructs a self-ordained minister, "Preach me a funeral sermon—a good one. Don't make me out no saint, but don't put me down too deep." Hogue desires, perhaps, precisely the sort of balance that Kristofferson's narrator strikes in *I'm Not There* when he "eulogizes" Dylan as "poet, prophet, outlaw, fake, star of electricity"—in short, some transcendent combination of "negative" and "positive" qualities. "There he lies," growls Kristofferson at the start of Haynes's film. "God rest his soul, and his rudeness. A devouring public can now share the remains of his sickness." (Kristofferson's narration freely quotes from Dylan's 1971 novel *Tarantula*, in which Dylan eulogizes himself, writing, "Here lies bob dylan / murdered / from behind / with trembling flesh." But Kristofferson also utters a line that appears in Charles Wright's poem "Stray Paragraphs in April, Year of the Rat," as well as in Greil Marcus's *Invisible Republic*: "Only the dead can be born again . . .")[78] Peckinpah's Hogue, hoping to be eulogized while still alive, explains, "It's not so much the dyin' that you hate—it's not knowin' what they're gonna *say* about you." Hogue is able to hear at least the first few lines of the minister's sermon: "Most funeral orations lie about a man—compare him to the angels, whitewash him with a very wide brush. . . . Now, a man's made out of bad as well as good—all of us. Cable Hogue came into this world, nobody knows when or where. He came stumbling out of the wilderness like a prophet of old." Such, of course, is the impression of Gere's Billy the Kid—and, by extension, of Dylan himself—that Haynes provides in *I'm Not There*. But it is also central to *Masked and Anonymous*, in which Val Kilmer's eccentric zookeeper observes of "man": "Who created him and for what purpose: still a mystery. Why is he here? It's a mystery. We know he's trespassing. Doesn't know his own place. . . . Masked and anonymous. No one truly knows 'im."

Time itself animates this mystery. When, during the opening credits of *I'm Not There*, Gere's Billy the Kid awakens with
a start—opens his eyes in an overhead shot—it is as if Rip
Van Winkle were waking, displaced and profoundly disori-
ented. By the end of the film, a relaxed Billy, having discovered
Woody's guitar—a gift from the future?—affirms his capacity
to combine tenses, to group "yesterday, today, and tomorrow
all in the same room." Nothing's lost forever. Precedents—and
presents—abound, if you know where to look for them. Anticipating *I'm Not There*, *Masked and Anonymous* has Luke Wilson's Bobby Cupid (Dylan as matchmaker?) discovering Blind
Lemon Jefferson's guitar, which he then, in a loving, reverent
gesture, hands over to Dylan's Jack Fate. But Blind Lemon's
guitar is more than just a fetish object to be passed from fan to
fan; its materiality remains substantial, and sufficiently deadly,
as Cupid demonstrates when he uses it to bludgeon a reporter
to death. The machine can kill fascists (or venal journalists),
but it destroys itself in the process. At the end of the scene,
there is nothing left of Blind Lemon's guitar but some ungodly
bits of wood.

SPEAKING FOR EDIE

Far from an arbitrary steal from Budd Schulberg, the term
"compost heap," with its connotations of growth from waste,
is thematically apt—a way of signaling the salvage operations
that Dylan and Haynes both undertake. As David Yaffe notes,
Dylan based "A Hard Rain's a-Gonna Fall" (1963), among
other major compositions, "on unused bits of other songs."[79]
Dylan's "associative writing," as Yaffe calls it, has definite
analogues in Haynes's filmmaking.[80] Yet if Dylan can freely

appropriate the work of others, why has it been so difficult
for others (with the conspicuous exception of Todd Haynes)
to appropriate the work of Dylan? A certain double standard
is evident in the discrepancy: Dylan polices without himself
being policed. Eugen Banauch has drawn attention to Dylan's
"strategies to regain a certain degree of autonomy over the
signifier Dylan, or to evade appropriations by others." Even
as Dylan "quotes, misquotes, and appropriates," he attempts
to enjoin others from doing the same.[81] Confronted with the
evidence of his own plagiarisms, Dylan, suddenly defensive,
sounds not unlike Haynes's sexist Robbie Clark, the "star of
electricity" who cruelly tells his feminist wife that "chicks"
are essentially insipid and "can never be poets." For Dylan,
only "wussies and pussies"—in a word, women—worry about
plagiarism (or "that stuff," as Dylan so dismissively calls it).[82]
In Dylan's misogynist imagination, complaining is easy—
feminine—while his own style of stealing, which targets the
work of other male artists (from Ezra Pound to Henry Timrod), is hard. Accordingly, Dylan threatens legal action against
those whose thefts are "easy" and "obvious"—and, as in the
case of *Factory Girl*, committed in the service of the feminine.

Haynes, of course, had far better luck with the Dylan camp,
but Dylan is not the only living subject referenced in *I'm Not
There*. Quite apart (but not always separable) from the law
are certain ethical questions that often plague the authors of
even the most oblique biographies. For Haynes, such questions
seemed to occur most insistently with respect to Suze Rotolo,
Dylan's long-ago girlfriend, whom the filmmaker anxiously
telephoned before the start of production. He admits that Rotolo "was worried about how she would be depicted," despite
Haynes's decision to refrain from actually naming her in the

film. Multiplied by Sara Dylan and given a new nationality, Rotolo became Charlotte Gainsbourg's Claire, a French expatriate who yet retains Rotolo's celebrated cultural connoisseurship. As Haynes put it, "You see this character turning [Robbie/Dylan] on to avant-garde theater. They're doing a live performance of *The Threepenny Opera* at this coffee shop. She's reading him Rimbaud and he's learning from this woman. So [Rotolo is] in the film even if she isn't literally cited."[83]

If Rotolo's approval eased Haynes's conscience, there was still Sara, Dylan's ex-wife, to consider. The British author and Dylan expert Michael Gray immediately recognized the potential breach of ethics represented by the sequence in which the marriage of Robbie and Claire breaks down: "As I watched the scenes between Gainsbourg and the Heath Ledger Bob (we know it's him by the sunglasses), I thought of the way the Bob-'n'-Sara divorce settlement bound her to lifelong silence and wondered how she might feel to see this Dylan-endorsed Hollywood movie sprawling their lives across the screen."[84] True to the terms of their divorce, Sara has remained mum on the subject of Bob Dylan—and, thus, on that of *I'm Not There*. Rotolo, however, apparently appreciated Haynes's decision to make Claire French.[85] In the film, the revelation of the character's nationality proves tremendously exciting to Robbie Clark, who blurts, "You're French. . . . That's perfect." It is perfect, certainly, for Robbie's masculine self-image, his status as a certain brand of heterosexual American man, automatically enamored of "Gallic" women. But it is also, in a way, perfect for Haynes—a sort of pretext for his homages to the French New Wave. Haynes, who studied with the film theorist Christian Metz in Paris, employs, for the Claire-and-Robbie segment, some of the formal strategies and technical standards that

Godard embraced in the 1960s, such as longer takes and wider angles. The result is a distinctly Godardian account of the end of love—akin, perhaps, to *Contempt* (1963), which Haynes further evokes with a circular pan around a statue. He also quotes directly from the script for Godard's *Masculin féminin*, reproducing Jean-Pierre Léaud's voice-over commentary on a certain spectatorial dissatisfaction: "It wasn't the movie of our dreams," Léaud's character says of a particular confection. "It wasn't the total film we carried inside ourselves." Haynes gives the speech—altered ever so slightly—to Ledger's Robbie, who delivers it in retrospective voice-over as the image track shows Robbie and Claire seated for the gala premiere of *Grain of Sand*, a staid biopic that proves tremendously disappointing, and that forms, perhaps, the first chink in the characters' relationship. (In Robbie's "omniscient" account, the disappointment is strictly Claire's.) Yet the "theft" is complicated by the fact that Godard himself stole the words, which derive from French novelist Georges Perec. "It is," observes Stephen Scobie, "thoroughly fitting that this high point of [Haynes's] film about Bob Dylan should be the unacknowledged quotation of an unacknowledged quotation."[86]

Though the Claire-and-Robbie section is formally distinct, all of *I'm Not There* features an aspect ratio of 2.40:1—a first for Haynes. "I was looking forward to a real reason for using widescreen," he said of the rectangular shape. "Some films are in anamorphic and there doesn't appear to be a valid reason—you just get the impression that the director thought it was cool. But it seemed absolutely necessary in this case, particularly for the landscape shots in the Billy the Kid sequences and the glimpses of trains in the beginning."[87] In *Contempt*, Fritz Lang, playing himself, complains of CinemaScope, "It's good only for snakes and funerals." But, much as it suits Godard's account of a marriage in crisis, it works remarkably well for Haynes's depiction of the same, particularly in scenes showing the growing horizontal distance between formerly conjoined lovers.

Dylan's litigiousness has often focused on attempts to narrate his romantic history—hardly surprising for someone whose divorce settlement imposed a lifelong gag order on his ex-wife. (Aggressively policing perceived libel, Dylan has nevertheless felt free to impugn others; in "Ballad in Plain D," he even refers to Suze Rotolo's sister Carla as a "parasite.") In his essay on *I'm Not There*, Greil Marcus writes that Heath Ledger and Charlotte Gainsbourg "act out a version of the romantic life of a real-life Bob Dylan who is now, already, no longer anything like the owner of his own story."[88] Yet he never was; one cannot own the facts of one's life, whatever the temporal span of that life. (Longevity has nothing to do with it.) The fact of Dylan's divorce, however personal and painful, was plainly free for the taking. And yet Dylan's aggressive policing of popular culture rendered this aspect of *I'm Not There* more startling, to some, than any other. As Gray pointed out upon the release of *I'm Not There*, "it's not long since Dylan's lawyers were leaning on the filming of George Hickenlooper's *Factory Girl* to try to stop anyone suggesting that he and Edie Sedgwick had a relationship, yet in *I'm Not There* [a] long sequence . . . has Bob and Edie center stage, the warring cool couple, young and thin and beautiful and, plain as studio lighting, in a relationship."[89] Gray, like many others, expressed surprise at Haynes's good fortune. How, exactly, was the filmmaker free to show the sadomasochistic charge of the Dylan-Sedgwick relationship when the creative personnel behind *Factory Girl* had been enjoined from suggesting that the two celebrities had ever even met? Compelled to change the name of Hayden Christensen's character from Bob Dylan to Billy Quinn, then informed through certified mail that such a change would not suffice, Hickenlooper, perhaps out of sheer frustration, finally decided to use no name at all. The lone word—"musician"— that appears in the closing credits functions as its own, cryptic index of the film's legal troubles, a bald affront to the man who threatened to sue.

Factory Girl was, in some senses, a victim of Dylan's legendary aggressiveness. Just a few years later, however, David Yaffe, in his book *Bob Dylan: Like a Complete Unknown* (2011), was free to ask, "What was [Dylan] looking for when he romanced Warhol Factory floozie Edie Sedgwick? Someone to discuss Chekhov with?" He followed this rather ungenerous assessment of Sedgwick—the flawed yet gifted heroine of *Factory Girl*, here reduced to unlettered dimensions by a seemingly reflexive misogyny—with a series of putative historical facts about "the couple": "Warhol introduced them, sort of. (A match made in the Factory! This would surely last.) Plus she was a beautiful, blond model and a drug addict. The relationship, needless to say, did not endure, but the songs it inspired certainly would, including 'Like a Rolling Stone,' 'Leopard Skin Pillbox Hat,' and 'Just Like a Woman.'" Dylan was, Yaffe continues, "no doubt motivated by Edie Sedgwick's empty yet alluring visage"—a fleeting fascination at best.[90] Is it possible that what upset Dylan about *Factory Girl* was the film's sheer compassion for its subject—the suggestion that he dumped not a mere "floozie" (as Yaffe has it) but a bold, bright, culturally curious survivor of sexual abuse? It is difficult to reconcile his attacks on *Factory Girl* with the carte blanche with which others have depicted "Bob and Edie." (Whatever else it is, *Factory*

Girl represents a love letter to Sedgwick.) Even *I'm Not There*
has characters dismissing Sedgwick—here named Coco Rivington and played by Michelle Williams—as "Andy's new girl"
and Jude's "little debutante," who fancies herself "queen of the
underground" (a term, and an accusation, taken from the Rolling Stones' distinctly Dylanesque song "Dead Flowers" [1971]).
"That girl's trouble," Jude warns. (Coco/Edie is referred to only
as a girl—never as a woman.) When she finally appears (outside of a cigarette ad glimpsed on the back of *Life* magazine),
it is as a sort of forest nymph offering oracular remarks: "You
might think nothing can reach those tens of thousands living
by the dollar. But you'd be wrong." (Is Coco here expressing
a Haynesian faith in the perceptual powers of the mass audience?) Jude, pursuing her through a thicket, immediately
apologizes: "I'm sorry about what happened." That much of the
ensuing exchange consists of quotations from Dylan's "She's
Your Lover Now"—an outtake from *Blonde on Blonde* that
shares a chord procession, and a certain misogynist thrust,
with "Like a Rolling Stone"—might suggest that Haynes is reverting to a rather familiar means of representing Sedgwick
(namely, via the innuendo of Dylan's own maligning lyrics).
Yet Coco has occasion to coolly dismiss Jude, saying, "Your
lucky tongue will not decay me." She also challenges his vanity:
"So that's what you think you have over everyone: freedom."
With a derisive laugh, she leaves him behind—to cough and
contemplate his drug-addled existence.

  In sharp contrast to Haynes's, Hickenlooper's production
was plagued by accusations of libel. Yet the muddled matter of authorship complicated even these claims. For Dylan's
legal team—his "pit bull lawyers," as the *New York Post* called
them—also sent a letter to Aaron Richard Golub, who was

Visions of Edie.

(and remains) credited only as cowriter of the story on which
Mauzner based his screenplay.[91] Who, then, was ultimately
responsible for the allegedly defamatory idea that Dylan had
not only "dumped" Sedgwick but also, in so doing, had driven
her to self-destruction? From whence had that idea come?
Was it "common knowledge"—as freely available for citation
as any element of the folk tradition on which Dylan had long
drawn? Or was it the invention of a single man—the product
of a distinctly creative mining of the rumor mill—who could
then be taken to court?

   If such questions were never adequately answered, they
still had material effects, including on *Factory Girl* itself. In
the finished film, Sienna Miller's Edie Sedgwick can be seen
mouthing Bob Dylan's name, but no corresponding sound can
be heard. The image track bears traces of the direct biographical approach—the explicit naming of Dylan—that the filmmakers had originally fashioned, but the final sound mix is
censorial. Simply put, the soundtrack falls silent when Miller,
as Sedgwick, says "Bob." The effect is odd—suggestive of a
workprint or other rough cut, as if the film, unfinished, and

certainly unpolished, were simply awaiting ADR. Acoustically, at least, the name "Bob Dylan" is not there, but its absence is conspicuous. It isn't spoken in Haynes's film, either, which uses a series of substitutes, from "Jack Rollins" to "Robbie Clark." If Hickenlooper had been forced to revise the shooting script— much as Haynes had been obliged to rewrite *Velvet Goldmine* over a nine-month period following David Bowie's refusal to license any of his songs to the production—he may well have missed the occasional "Bob," the odd "Dylan."[92] Yet the Dylan persona is very much available in Christensen's performance. Even the dialogue suggests a Dylan interview. Asked what he is "trying to say" with his songs, Christensen's character offers a most Dylanesque answer: "I'm not trying to say anything. I just write 'em. I guess I just write about what I see." ("I seem to draw into myself whatever comes my way, and it comes out of me," Dylan told *Seventeen*, the first major magazine to profile him, in 1962.)[93] Later, he quarrels with Sedgwick, who accuses him of "pretending to be some sort of crusader." "What exactly is the message," she continues, "aside from 'Look at me'?" Calling him an "overpaid prophet," she articulates some of the objections to Dylan voiced throughout the latter half of the 1960s by journalists and members of the folk community, for whom "selling out" was still the gravest of sins. Yet *Factory Girl*, which features a famously scathing depiction of Andy Warhol (played by a petulant Guy Pearce), ultimately redeems Dylan, placing him decisively on the side of "depth" and "truth." After reluctantly submitting to a *Screen Test*, he forces Sedgwick to make a choice: live with him in Woodstock or remain a "disposable prop" in Warhol's Factory.

Dylan is thus the crux of the melodrama—the potential savior whose offer, a kind of lifeline, eventually expires. By

the time Sedgwick comes to her senses and excoriates Warhol
as a "faggot" who has "made a fool out of" her, it is too late:
Dylan has found and married his "sweet love," Sara. (In an
apparent gaffe, the newspaper clipping that apprises Edie of
the wedding identifies Christensen's character as "folk singer
Tommy Quinn"; elsewhere, his name is written as "Billy," while
the actors mouth "Bob"—a mélange of labels that does little to
distract from Christensen's resemblance to Dylan, much as, in
I'm Not There, no alias—not "Jack Rollins," not "Jude Quinn"—
can diminish Dylan's iconic and phonetic availability.) In his
DVD commentary, Hickenlooper talks about some of the
many parallels between what he refers to as "Todd Haynes's
new movie" and *Factory Girl*.[94] The two films shared costume
designer John Dunn, who worked on them more or less simultaneously and to strikingly equivalent ends. Both productions
utilized Super 8: Tanya Smith, Haynes's friend and assistant,
shot Super 8 color footage of Montreal playing Greenwich
Village, while Hickenlooper's team shot Super 8 color footage of Shreveport playing Midtown Manhattan. (Hurricane
Katrina had forced *Factory Girl* out of New Orleans, the film's
original shooting location.) Both productions also made use
of Super 16, which, in addition to lightweight cameras that
could easily be wielded by hand, offered a grain similar to what
35-millimeter exhibited in the sixties. (Haynes, whose budget
was about three times that of Hickenlooper's, was also able to
use Super 35.) *Factory Girl* and *I'm Not There* both faithfully
re-create various photographs, interviews, press conferences,
and film scenes. The former exactingly reproduces Warhol's
Beauty No. 2 (1965), down to the precise aspect ratio (3:4) and
the use of black-and-white reversal stock. Elsewhere in *Factory
Girl*, the use of a 90-degree shutter produces a slightly flick-

ering image—a historiographical as much as a mood-setting, tension-generating gesture, a jarring effect that Haynes achieves in parts of *Superstar* and *I'm Not There*, as well as in the documentary *The Velvet Underground* (2021), which draws on archival images to explore the Factory scene in some detail.

Even as he (rightly) emphasizes the similarities between *Factory Girl* and *I'm Not There* (which also shared a North American distributor, the Weinstein Company), Hickenlooper cannot help but pepper his DVD commentary with justified complaints about something that Haynes did not experience— namely, Dylan's juridical interference, his legal policing. Enjoined from identifying Dylan by name, Hickenlooper speaks at length about "one person in particular who has been extremely aggressive in trying to take down our picture for his own reasons—a guy [who] has profited off of Edie's memory quite a bit himself." (With this last assertion, Hickenlooper is seemingly repeating the popular assumption that at least a few of Dylan's most famous, indeed profitable, songs are about Sedgwick.) Hickenlooper even echoes Haynes's take on *I'm Not There* when he says of *Factory Girl*, "It's not a traditional biopic." Dylan's legal threats continued to constrain Hickenlooper long after the film's theatrical release. When he recorded the DVD commentary, there were two lawyers standing next to him in the sound booth, making sure that he wouldn't speak Dylan's name. "I can't get into detail for legal reasons," he explains on the DVD, but Dylan is there anyway, the obvious if unnamed subject of his most scathing remarks.[95]

The strange case of *Factory Girl* appeared to have been forgotten by the time *I'm Not There* was released in the fall of 2007, just eleven months after Dylan's lawyers first contacted the Weinstein Company. Yet rather than the principled antithesis of the much-maligned *Factory Girl*, Haynes's *I'm Not There* duplicates many of the other film's devices, including the use of the name "Quinn" as a metonym for Dylan. (Hayden Christensen's "Billy Quinn" becomes Cate Blanchett's "Jude Quinn.") *I'm Not There* even has its own Edie Sedgwick, in the aforementioned form of Michelle Williams's "Coco Rivington," whom Blanchett's Quinn subjects to far more vitriol, misogynist and otherwise, than Christensen's Dylan figure ever levels against the protagonist of *Factory Girl*. Legally enforceable constraints on representation had hindered Hickenlooper and his associates, forcing them to apply various pseudonyms to their project and to temper any suggestion that Dylan was unfair to Sedgwick, whether in the flesh or through his acidic lyrics. But Haynes, too, used aliases, even for the long-deceased Sedgwick. His depiction of "Jude's" raw, corrosive final encounter with "Coco" is far less cautious than anything in *Factory Girl*: it suggests not simply that Dylan and Sedgwick had sex but that the former emotionally abused the latter; the altercation ends with Williams's Sedgwick stand-in fleeing the scene of her humiliation, her carefully cultivated armor—the veneer of the imperturbable party girl—having cracked with a blood-curdling scream at Jude's hostility.

In the spring of 2007, after Dylan had seemingly lost interest in the little-seen *Factory Girl*, Harvey Weinstein viewed the first cut of *I'm Not There*, and he was reasonably pleased with the result—and, perhaps, convinced that the film could not possibly offend Dylan, if only because it seemed so inscrutable. "I may have emphasized the obscurity factor in order to quell any suspicions on the part of my subject regarding rampant exploitation," Haynes admitted.[96] Still, Weinstein had a few objections, including to Richard Gere's Billy the Kid, whose segment, the executive concluded, was unclear and unnecessary.[97] In his initial negotiations with the Weinstein Company, Haynes had managed to acquire the right to final cut, which gave him the power to ignore Harvey's concerns.[98] As Thomas Doherty puts it, "To possess final cut is to wrest ownership and assert authorship: to sign off on the film before the negative is duplicated and the prints are circulated. Whatever corporate entity bankrolls the project, the auteur with final cut certifies the film as a finished *objet d'art* stamped with a proprietary credit and personal signature."[99] Doherty's language may appear to conflate forms of control—creative and legal—that are usually decidedly separate, but his account of final cut is an apt summation of why, and how, *I'm Not There* is, in the end, very much a film by Todd Haynes (even if he doesn't own it). With domestic distribution in the hands of the Weinstein Company, *I'm Not There* suffered at least as much neglect as had *Velvet Goldmine.* "I didn't feel he understood or particularly supported [*I'm Not There*]," Cate Blanchett would later say of Harvey Weinstein.[100] Of course, being Blanchett, she proceeded to subtly demonstrate *her* understanding of the film, about a dozen years after it was shot: asked about the tiny bronze harmonica hanging on a chain around her neck, she replied, "I played Bob Dylan, but I cannot play the harmonica"—before improvising a variation on the harmonica part in "Mr. Tambourine Man" that beautifully echoed the actual Dylan performance that concludes *I'm Not There.* Breathing in and out through the instrument, Blanchett, for a brief moment, became Dylan once again.

Mock the Documentary

Dont Look Back, which captures a few weeks of Dylan's 1965 tour of the UK, has been an object of parody practically since its premiere. Released alongside *I'm Not There*, Jake Kasdan's *Walk Hard: The Dewey Cox Story* (2007), a spoof of musical biopics, similarly draws on Pennebaker's film (via *No Direction Home*) in a sequence in which the chameleonic title character (played by John C. Reilly), well into the "finger-pointing" phase of his career, is repeatedly compared to Bob Dylan. "It's 1966," he tells his wife (played by Jenna Fischer), who replies with a parody of historiographical shorthand: "The sixties are an important and exciting time!" The film then transitions into a black-and-white re-creation of one of the 1965 press conferences that Pennebaker's cameras captured. In approximating the vérité style of *Dont Look Back*, *Walk Hard* also mirrors *I'm Not There*, with Reilly, seated at a long table and blinking before the flashbulbs, standing in for Cate Blanchett. Fittingly, Kasdan's reproduction pivots around the question of imitation, as journalists charge Cox with having "stolen" his style. "Some people are saying that your new music sounds a lot like Bob Dylan," says one reporter (who, incidentally, bears a passing resemblance to Bruce Greenwood's Mr. Jones). "Well maybe Bob Dylan sounds a lot like me!" Cox responds. "You know, how come nobody ever asks Bob Dylan, 'Why do you sound so much like Dewey Cox?'" The film thus alludes to a moment in *No Direction Home* in which an amused Dave Van Ronk explains that, after Dylan borrowed Van Ronk's version of the traditional folk song "House of the Rising Sun" (chord changes and all), Van Ronk was accused of copying *Dylan*—of imitating his imitator—whenever he dared to play it. Dylan, too, would eventually fall victim to the public's misapprehension of the temporal order of things, Van Ronk notes with a laugh: after the Animals scored a massive hit with *their* version of the song, people started accusing Dylan of having stolen it from *them*. When *Walk Hard*, still suggesting *Dont Look Back* through its period mise-en-scène and handheld cinematography, shows Cox performing one of his "protest" songs, he sounds, of course, deeply Dylanseque. Like Blanchett's Jude, he looks the part, too, his tangled hair its own emblem of the era. That he also resembles Bale's Jack Rollins is a function of the films' shared source in the Scorsese documentary: footage of the young Dylan performing in a Mississippi cotton field is faithfully reproduced in both *Walk Hard* and *I'm Not There*. Exactly contemporaneous, the films are also, at times, uncannily similar, not just visually but also, given the occasionally satiric spirit of Haynes's work, tonally, too.

The temptation to lampoon Dylan had, of course, long been available to filmmakers. Released on the eve of the Clinton presidency, Tim Robbins's *Bob Roberts* is another spoof of Dylan, though the star's name is never actually uttered.[1] (*Bob Roberts* is, in this way, closer to *I'm Not There* than to *Walk Hard*: Dylan is at once everywhere and nowhere.) Played by Robbins, the title character, a right-wing millionaire whose success as a folk singer paves the way for his headline-generating senatorial campaign, is Dylan's musical double, if not necessarily his political twin. Roberts's 1987 debut album, *The Freewheelin' Bob Roberts*—described by critics as "a corrupt, unfair diatribe against the sixties"—has a cover that duplicates that of Dylan's second studio album, *The Freewheelin' Bob Dylan* (1963). A subsequent Roberts album, *Times Are Changin' Back*, features songs like "Retake America" and "Wall Street Rap." Included in the hybridic *Bob Roberts*, a promotional video for the latter track imitates the long pretitle take—itself inspired by the short musical films shown in coin-operated "movie jukeboxes"—that, scored to "Subterranean Homesick Blues," opens *Dont Look Back*.[2] Like Dylan in the Pennebaker documentary, Roberts holds a stack of cue cards on which snippets of song lyrics are scrawled. (The video-within-the-film also manages to spoof Robert Palmer: the backup dancers are as sprucely dressed as Roberts, thus evoking the iconic music video for 1985's "Addicted to Love.") The character's appropriation of Dylan is more than mere aesthetic imitation, however, and *Bob Roberts*, anticipating *I'm Not There*, investigates the seamier side of chronic self-invention. To affect some of Dylan's preferred locutions (themselves borrowed from his own mentors and idols): when you ain't got no politics, you might just end up an ultra-conservative mouthpiece (as Robbie Clark surely does in *I'm Not There*, suddenly adopting a sexist, gender-essentialist line of argument, much to Claire's disgust and dismay). Roberts embraces what he takes to be the prototypically American promise of "self-determination"—"the choice to be what you want to be," as he puts it to an enthusiastic audience at one of his concerts. "And I wanted to be *rich*," he adds (and the crowd roars). Earlier in the film, Lynne Thigpen's principled television reporter sums up the sociopathic Roberts: "Here is a man who has adopted

the persona and mindset of the freethinking rebel and turned
it on itself: the rebel conservative. *That* is deviant brilliance.
What a Machiavellian poseur!" In a parody of *Eat the Document*, Robbins depicts interviews (conducted by a British filmmaker at work on a documentary on Roberts) with disgruntled
young men and women who vent their frustrations outside
the various concert halls where the politician is playing. But
such figures, however angry, have little effect on the election.
Roberts is as impervious to their complaints as the Dylan who,
throughout *Eat the Document*, blithely dismisses the earnest
questions of various reporters.

Recalling the Robert Drew Associates film *Primary* (1960),
made for the television branch of Time-Life, *Bob Roberts* also
anticipates *The War Room*, Chris Hegedus and D. A. Pennebaker's 1993 documentary about the Clinton campaign. But its
affinities with *I'm Not There* suggest that it is more than just
a takeoff of a certain style of "political" documentary. It is not
incidental that Dylan is the source of inspiration for Roberts
(and Robbins). There were, by the early 1990s, plenty of other
rock stars to spoof, just as there were documentaries at least
as recognizable—as iconic—as *Dont Look Back* (because made
very much in its influential vein). But Robbins chose Dylan, for
reasons that might not be all that far from Haynes's. "I loved
the way that Dylan kept reinventing himself at a time that
was very different from the self-consciousness of the Bowie
era (reflected in *Velvet Goldmine*)," Haynes has said. "This was
a period giddy with authenticity and 'truth'—the Civil Rights
era (my God, it doesn't get any realer than that). But the more
Dylan changed, the more authentic he appeared. And the more
he tried to shuck off all the prescriptive politics and pressure
and expectation, the more pivotal were the realizations he

engendered."[3] Yet *Bob Roberts* reveals just how easily such practiced apoliticism can slip into distinctly reactionary territory. So, of course, does *I'm Not There*, particularly in Ledger's scenes as Robbie Clark. "There are no politics," Robbie says, mere seconds after declaring (celebrating?) the defeat of leftism ("Face it: it's over") and proclaiming the legitimacy of biological misogyny ("Guys and chicks are different. . . . Chicks can never be poets"). Robbie's politics not only exist, despite his protestations to the contrary; they are also—plainly—the politics of exclusion and discrimination. Like Bob Roberts, he might even hold them for good, having forgotten the sentiments encapsulated in songs once performed by his most famous character—Jack Rollins—which include "The Lonesome Death of Hattie Carroll," a wrenching denunciation of the violent misogyny of white supremacy ("William Zanzinger killed poor Hattie Carroll / With a cane that he twirled around his diamond ring finger . . ."). Even the title of Robbie's starring vehicle *Grain of Sand*—a Jack Rollins biopic—suggests the actor's selfishness and isolation, a singularity that sharply contrasts with the communitarian inclusiveness implied in the title of Dylan's gospel number "Every Grain of Sand," the final track on *Shot of Love* (1981). Jack Rollins, of course, avoids Robbie's lonely fate by joining the Pentecostal collective. Julianne Moore's Alice Fabian says that Rollins stopped protesting in 1963, but Robbie never started.

Dylan, for his part, did not publicly endorse a presidential candidate until 2008, when he threw his support behind Barack Obama, saying of the politician, "He's like a fictional character, but he's real."[4] Obama's tangible qualities—constitutive of his "realness"—were not, however, guarantees against political disillusionment, any more than were the phenomenal premises of any previous presidency. As Dylan sings in "Political World," a 1989 song later featured in Barry Levinson's political satire *Man of the Year* (2006), "We live in a political world / The one we can see and feel / But there's no one to check, it's all a stacked deck / We all know for sure that it's real." Recognizing reality is not the same as exercising autonomy over it; a game is no less real for being rigged. ("The *system* is *rigged*," insists Mark Ruffalo's crusading attorney in Haynes's *Dark Waters*. "They want us to think that it'll protect us, but that's a lie.") Yet "real" is still a rather curious word for an artist like Dylan to use; it certainly has little purchase in the fantastical *I'm Not There*. (When he says of the civil rights movement that "it doesn't get any realer than that," what, exactly, does Todd Haynes mean?) On election night in 2008, appearing at a packed concert in Minneapolis, Dylan told his fans, "I was born in 1941—that's the year they bombed Pearl Harbor. Well, I been livin' in a world of darkness ever since. But it looks like things are gonna change now."[5] That Obama—a master of war as formidable as any Dylan had ostensibly denounced in song—would only strengthen the American military-industrial state, authorizing more drone strikes in his first year than his predecessor had in his entire presidency, is something that Dylan could not perhaps have predicted. Yet his folksy autobiographical musings, offered (whether "truthfully" or in jest) on that historic night in 2008, neatly summarize the logic of national security that undergirds the modern American presidency: "they" are threatening to "darken" the world over which the United States has, reputedly, every right to preside.

Just as Haynes unearthed "I'm Not There" for his film of that name, Robbins, sensing the need to inject some hope into the otherwise bleakly funny *Bob Roberts*, resurrected a reel-to-reel audiotape recording of an obscure Woody Guthrie song—"I've Got to Know" (ca. 1948), which plays, in all its scratchy glory, over the film's end credits, a sonic balm after Roberts's synthetic folk. Guthrie's daughter Nora shared the reel-to-reel tape—one of her own archival discoveries, recorded in a hotel room some forty years before—giving Robbins permission to use "I've Got to Know" in a film that lampoons one of Guthrie's actual heirs and, in so doing, raises questions about his "apolitical" style and estrangement from protest songs.[6] For if "A Hard Rain's a-Gonna Fall" *isn't* political, then what is it—fodder for the likes of Bob Roberts, something to be requisitioned by the right, the sonic model for a certain brand of conservatism? (As Pauline Kael observed in 1978, nearly two years after Dylan stopped performing the ostensible protest song "Hurricane," "one can never be sure whether Dylan means what he says.")[7] In *Eat the Document*, Dylan merely waves his hand in dismissal of the question "Are you ever yourself at any time?" But he bluntly responds to a reporter's attempt to explain why so many are upset with him. "When," the reporter says, "an image is projected on something which we feel is particularly serious, and then, if you become cynical about it, one begins to doubt sincerity." "I'm not sincere at all," Dylan answers, casting even "The Lonesome Death of Hattie Carroll" as phony. *Bob Roberts* brings in the actual Woody Guthrie as if to exorcise not simply the title character but also the roguish Dylan himself.

The parallels between *Bob Roberts* and *I'm Not There* do not end with these musical rescue missions. In the fall of 2020, Robbins recalled his run-ins with Harvey Weinstein, who acquired *Bob Roberts* at Cannes, eventually distributing the film through Paramount. "I can't tell you how many phone calls I got from Harvey Weinstein trying to get me to cut this or cut that, change this or change that," Robbins said. "But I had final cut."[8] Like Haynes with *I'm Not There*, Robbins was able to maintain autonomy over his work even in the face of so fearsome a power broker as Harvey Weinstein. As a result, the latter can hardly be said to have supported *Bob Roberts*, which disappeared from theaters even faster than Haynes's film—and made even less.

A PASTICHE FOR TV

The inspiration for numerous sequences in *I'm Not There*, Dylan's elusive *Eat the Document* did not have to contend with the likes of Harvey Weinstein—or, for that matter, with any distribution company at all. The film is a fractured record of Dylan and the Hawks' 1966 tour of Europe. (Later known as the Band, the Hawks provided backup for Dylan during this period.) Shot under Dylan's direction by D. A. Pennebaker, *Eat the Document* includes snippets of Dylan performing, among other songs, "Tell Me, Momma," "I Don't Believe You (She Acts Like We Never Met)," and "Ballad of a Thin Man." "It is a chaotic film," writes Sean Wilentz, "that appears to be about chaos, in the spirit of Rimbaud's derangement of the senses."[9] ABC originally commissioned *Eat the Document* for its throwback anthology series *ABC Stage 67* (1966–1967), but the network allegedly ended up rejecting what it saw of the film before the series itself was canceled in the spring of 1967. Reputedly "confused by its stream-of-consciousness organization" and simply "not ready for Dylan's impressionistic, experimental work," ABC surrendered the project to him.[10]

The film's journey to its "rejection" by commercial television was hardly a simple one, however, and it complicates the conventional explanation that Dylan was ultimately "too radical" for a major broadcast network—a cliché that, of course, flatters Dylan while failing to attend to the particulars of the case. For one thing, *ABC Stage 67* was itself a proto-Haynesian pastiche, meant to mix modes, genres, and styles in a prime-time format promoted as homage to a period of television history that, though recent, could seem all but unrecoverable in the late 1960s: that of the "Golden Age" of anthology programming, which began its much-lamented decline in the mid-1950s. (Ironically, ABC, which merged with United Paramount Theaters in 1953 and was an early, enthusiastic adopter of Hollywood-produced telefilm series, had a reputation as the architect of the demise of "prestige" TV.)[11] As the network's president promised a congressional subcommittee in the spring of 1966 (when Dylan was on his European tour), *ABC Stage 67* would be "an innovational hour[-long] program"—a "tremendously risky affair," with a different independent producer for each week's show. Previous experience in television production was not a prerequisite for working on *ABC Stage 67*, each of whose hours was to "have some innovative aspects to it."[12] The unorthodox Dylan was commissioned precisely for his potential to disturb some of the representational methods that had succeeded the so-called Golden Age and replaced its putatively vital heterogeneity with a sterility that many associated with the production in Hollywood of cheap, genre-bound, continuing-character series shot on film. Seemingly overnight, the Golden Age—a victim of emergent economic imperatives and of inadequate federal regulation—had, critics complained, given way to a "Vast Wasteland" of uninspired programming.[13]

When ABC's president testified before Congress in the spring of 1966, he was obliged to address, as part of a major regulatory investigation, the question of commercial television's capacity to accommodate small-scale independent production. *ABC Stage 67* was offered, however cynically and strategically, as evidence of the network's renewed commitment to "offbeat" programming.

The approach worked. Anthology drama, which, William Boddy points out, had been "a jewel in the networks' public relations crown during a time of public scrutiny" in the 1950s, was again trotted out to show just how seriously ABC took its public-service mandate.[14] Congressman John D. Dingell, expressing gratitude for the network president's testimony, and perhaps moved by the latter's nostalgic evocation of television's Golden Age, thanked him for having "made a very fine statement." "We think," Dingell continued, "that you have a company of which you can be very proud, and one which indeed is very forward-looking in terms of its operation."[15] Regulatory concerns were thus allayed at the very moment at which Dylan, working as an inexperienced and altogether unconventional independent producer for ABC, was in Europe shooting what would become *Eat the Document*. One of Dylan's biographers, Howard Sounes, describes him as "naively thinking he could create an experimental film between touring commitments," but it was this "naiveté"—coupled, of course, with Dylan's outsize celebrity—that had attracted ABC in the first place.[16] From the network's perspective, hiring Dylan was a way of hedging its bets: his status as an independent producer—someone from outside the American television industry—could be cited as evidence of ABC's commitment to "diversity" and "innovation," while his fame could ensure that, whatever he came up with, people would feel compelled to tune in for it.

Postproduction was soon interrupted by Dylan's motorcycle accident (or "incident," as Sounes calls it) in the summer of 1966, mere weeks after the events that Pennebaker's cameras had recorded. Sounes suggests that the occurrence, the particulars of which have "remained extraordinarily mysterious," was "not as serious as was reported at the time." It was, in any case, "very convenient for Bob," as it "gave [him] an excuse to get out of the numerous business commitments then threatening to overwhelm him."[17] Indeed, *ABC Stage 67* could not outlast his retreat from the public eye. After "fully recuperating," Dylan proceeded to cut *Eat the Document* himself, with help from Howard Alk (whom Greil Marcus credits as codirector of the film) and with equipment supplied by Pennebaker.[18] The latter, sounding not unlike the Robbie Clark who, in *I'm Not There*, condescendingly warns Claire that a motorbike is "not a fucking can of tomatoes," averred that film editing is "not something you learn parking cars in a garage. You gotta know some of the rules."[19] That Dylan did not know—or deliberately broke—those rules is evident from his "final" cut of *Eat the Document*, which, while at times incomprehensible, is no more so than many of the celebrated works of avant-garde or "underground" cinema of its era. At times, the preponderance of jump cuts suggests not ignorance of film form but obeisance to the French New Wave. In *I'm Not There*, Claire confounds Robbie's condescension with her competence on the motorbike (she literally rides circles around him), and Dylan, too, perhaps disproved Pennebaker's point by picking up certain skills as a film editor. While *Eat the Document* is hardly beholden to the system of continuity editing, its distance from such norms seems precisely the point. Dylan's confusion of spatial and temporal coordinates represents a deliberate choice.

Executives at ABC may well have disliked what Dylan reportedly showed them (though no one has ever been able to prove that he showed them *anything*), but the eventual completion—and copyrighting—of *Eat the Document* in 1971 postdated the cancellation of *ABC Stage 67* by nearly four years. It is misleading to suggest that what has since been available for public viewing, whether through bootleg cassettes or museum screenings, was necessarily "unsuitable" for network television. If anything was incompatible with the demands of the medium in the late 1960s, it was the nostalgic *ABC Stage 67*, which received consistently low ratings. An ill-fated attempt to recapture something of the heyday of *The Philco Television Playhouse* (1948–1955) and *Westinghouse Studio One* (1948–1958), *ABC Stage 67* was off the air long before Dylan left the editing table.

Having lost its berth at ABC, *Eat the Document* "languished on the shelf" until New York's Academy of Music and the Whitney Museum of Art held special screenings in the early 1970s.[20] Bootleg tapes (and, later, VCDs, DVDs, and video files) gave it additional, "underground," life. (In 2000, while outlining *I'm Not There*, Haynes was able to rent a bootleg copy of *Eat the Document* from Movie Madness, the legendary Portland video store.)[21] Scorsese edited parts of it into *No Direction Home*, thereby demonstrating the historical but also aesthetic value of the work. Heightening Scorsese's homage, *I'm Not There* ends with two excerpts from *Eat the Document*, both of them reframed—cropped—to conform to the film's super-widescreen aspect ratio: a handheld tracking shot, slightly shorter in Haynes's film than in Dylan's, of sprucely dressed young people gathered outdoors at dusk; and a smooth long take (again, somewhat shorter in *I'm Not There* than in *Eat the Document*) of Dylan, in close-up, playing the harmonica. The first shot suggests, in both films, that the young people are congregating for a Dylan performance. In *Eat the Document*, "Mr. Tambourine Man" is faintly audible on the soundtrack (Dylan can be heard, as if in the distance, his voice made tinnier by a shoddy PA system, singing one of the song's verses), though none of the young people seem to take notice of it. Indeed, this may well be a kind of mismatch, the product of a creative, deceptive joining of image and sound, or simply a sort of aural preview, however subtle, of a performance to come. The posh youths stand as if in anticipation of something. Many look directly at the camera as it smoothly penetrates the crowd, plainly more concerned with its insistent presence than with the sounds that—for the film's audience, at least—accompany them. Perhaps they are waiting not for Dylan but for someone else. (*Eat the Document* includes footage of crowds assembled for, among other events, a public performance of the Band of the Royal Regiment of Scotland; Dylan is not, the film repeatedly shows, the only musical attraction in Europe.) In *I'm Not There*, a sound bridge, consisting of snatches of Dylan's improvised elaborations on the harmonica part in "Mr. Tambourine Man," links the mobile shot of the crowd to the equally penetrating close-up of the artist and his instrument, the two looming ever larger via the use of a zoom lens. In visual terms, this marks a sudden transition from day to night, from the lowering but still-piercing light of dusk to the darkness of a nocturnal (or simply enclosed) performance, black except for Dylan's precisely spotlighted face.

In *Eat the Document*, by contrast, the two images do not

appear in immediate succession but are separated by several shots of Dylan's backstage preparations, which include his interacting with various members of his entourage. Trimming this interstitial fat, *I'm Not There* distills a certain "essence" of the Dylan persona (circa 1966), one reducible to youthful fandom (the shot of the crowd suggests something out of the television series *Mad Men*, whose first season, exactly contemporaneous with Haynes's film, ended with Dylan's "Don't Think Twice, It's All Right") and enigmatic musicianship. Dylan's unbroken harmonica melody moves in one tuneful direction, reverses course with a sudden, wheezy whine—a jarring, atonal interruption—and finally returns to the original mellifluous refrain. Haynes, aiming for a valedictory effect, imposes a fadeout on the image. *Eat the Document* simply cuts, after nearly two minutes, to a different angle on Dylan, and then, once he has stopped playing and has taken his bow, to a new scene, which begins with a shot through the windshield of the car taking Dylan and John Lennon through the rain-soaked streets of London. As used at the very end of *I'm Not There*, the low-angle close-up of Dylan playing the harmonica slowly disappears, diminishing by degrees, along with the sound of his music (though Dylan does not, as in *Eat the Document*, stop playing). As soon as the screen is completely black, Haynes's dedication—"in memory of JIM LYONS"—appears. "Like a Rolling Stone," Dylan's magnum opus, kicks in immediately thereafter.

If the Scorsese documentary seemed to validate *Eat the Document*, Haynes's film would pay it an even greater tribute, giving it the last word, as it were. The specifically cinematic qualities of Dylan's work—so obvious in *I'm Not There*—have long been apparent to Dylan scholars. Seth Rogovoy calls *Eat*

the Document "Dylan's first real effort as a filmmaker, his first
attempt at capturing in the film medium that he grew up with
and which was as close to his heart as music the same sort of
expressionism he explored in song."[22] Sounes says that Dylan
"wanted to improvise scenes in the style of an art film," though
Sounes is perhaps uncharitable toward the results, reliant as
he is on the embittered assessments of Dylan's former associates.[23] No fan of *Eat the Document*, Pennebaker explained to
Sounes that the title meant, to Dylan, "a nondocumentary."[24]
Indeed, the film represents a sort of repudiation of the grammar of cinéma vérité (and thus of Pennebaker's own *Dont
Look Back*). It is, for one thing, resolutely nonlinear, legible
as a concert film only in fits and starts (and then only partially), its near-constant jump cuts and general resistance to
any sort of spatiotemporal clarity a clear provocation (like the
harsh metallic wail that briefly interrupts Dylan's otherwise
soothing variations on "Mr. Tambourine Man"). Anyone ex-
pecting vérité-style "revelations"—of Dylan's "true" character,
or simply of the relationship of one shot to another—will be
sorely disappointed. Greil Marcus suggests that *Eat the Document*, however "disrespectful" of certain documentary aesthet-
ics, retains considerable documentary value—precisely what
Scorsese, paving the way for Haynes's own appropriations,
would draw upon, and thus sanctify, in *No Direction Home*.
Marcus calls *Eat the Document* "an inspired jumble of shots
and situations, sometimes re-creating the performance of a
single song with footage from numerous [European] performances; ultimately, the war between the musicians and their
audiences comes into full relief."[25] That last phrase is, however,
a bit excessive—symptomatic, perhaps, of the lingering desire,
conditioned by cinéma vérité, to receive as "revelatory" any

documentation of public performance.

Indeed, the supposed "war between musicians and their audiences" was a central concern of cinéma vérité, in which concert films like Pennebaker's *Monterey Pop* (1968) and the Maysles brothers' *Gimme Shelter* (1970) had pride of place. As Jonathan Kahana notes, the vérité style of such rock documentaries "was intended to recreate the experience of being there"; they invariably "invited the viewer's participation" in the community of concertgoers whose musical experiences the films so "artlessly" recorded.[26] Certainly there is nothing "intimate" or "inviting" about *Eat the Document*, which, rather than "mystifying" cinematic production, renders conspicuous the apparent arduousness with which it was made and edited, transposing the pain of creation into the discomfort of confused spectatorship. "For all its spontaneity and 'uncontrolled' energy," Kahana concludes, "the *cinéma vérité* documentary style was not so different, as a vision of society, an evocation of a community of viewers, from the classical documentary it claimed to replace."[27] Marcus's offhand description of *Eat the Document*, which applies more to the antisymbolic earnestness in which Kahana implicates vérité, is ultimately more misleading than accounts that complain of the film's off-putting elements and the sheer indeterminacy of its "meanings." The eventual incorporation of the film into Scorsese's PBS documentary might, then, suggest a certain taming—the assimilation of *Eat the Document* into the very style that Dylan had sought to undo. But its use in *I'm Not There*, which shares its destabilizing spirit, is certainly no domestication, even as Haynes performs his own veneration of the interpolated footage, and of Dylan, on whose face he slowly fades out.

Discussing *Eat the Document* with Richard Porton, Haynes

appeared to align the film with cinéma vérité, endorsing the
style's association with self-exposure while also naming its uni-
versalizing ambitions: "There are moments when the veneer
of any famous performer—it doesn't have to be Dylan—cracks
and you see the real pulse or essence of the guy and say, 'That's
what makes him special.' You don't get the icon that hangs on
the mantle but an inkling of the real creature."[28] Elsewhere,
Haynes said of the "openness" of *I'm Not There*, "[Dylan's] essence [is] depicted as many individuals, with clashing views
and different perspectives, which I think is the way any of us
would prefer seeing ourselves, rather than as some single person with a perfect arc."[29] Haynes also indicates the heterogeneity of Dylan's audiences even as he emphasizes the popular
rage with which the artist's "electrification" was met. This, too,
is rooted in *Eat the Document*, which, in addition to offering
ample evidence of concertgoers' discontent, records a few dissenting voices. "Actually, it's quite nice—I rather enjoyed it,"
one clean-cut young British man tells Pennebaker's camera. ("I
kinda liked getting blasted out of my skin," says a lone defender
of Jude's combative festival performance in *I'm Not There*.)
Others, echoing Pete Seeger's objection to the sound levels and
related electronic distortions at Newport in 1965, complain of
Dylan's incomprehensibility: "You couldn't hear a single word
he was saying!" The same claim could easily be made of the
dissonant *Eat the Document*, with its variable sound quality
and often-mumbling onscreen subjects. At times, however,
a dialectic of abuse and appreciation emerges from the vox-
populi interviews, particularly when audience members openly
disagree with one another. One young Brit says that Dylan's
concert was "rubbish," but another interrupts him to say, "I
think Bob Dylan's the greatest—every time. Every time." Yet

these reception strategies are intercut with Dylan's abrasive performance of "Like a Rolling Stone," which Scorsese would include in *No Direction Home*, and which here seems intended to explain, if not endorse, the enmity of certain parties.

The apparent spontaneity of the audience responses included in *Eat the Document* is enhanced by their spatial and temporal proximity to Dylan's live concerts. Pennebaker recorded individuals as they emerged from various auditoria, some of them after the concerts had ended, others while Dylan was still performing inside. These person-on-the-street interviews constituted a style so familiar that it was frequently parodied even at the time, as in Peter Watkins's *The War Game* (1965). Along with the concert footage, they represented by far the most conventional elements of *Eat the Document*, and it is no surprise that they were recycled in Scorsese's *No Direction Home*, itself a rather standard combination of contemporary interviews and archival elements. *No Direction Home* steers mostly clear of the jump cuts and other avant-garde techniques evident in *Eat the Document*, which offers multiple documentary modes. These discrepant documentary styles are approximated throughout Haynes's work, in which they often serve competing functions. The exploitative epistemic drive of *Superstar*'s voice-over narrator ("What happened?" he demands at the outset) is plainly at odds with the film's more sober, "intellectual" accounts of consumerism and anorexia nervosa; the intervening talking heads, who evaluate Karen Carpenter's musical gifts (thus prefiguring the expert witnesses who, in *I'm Not There*, address Jack Rollins's strengths and weaknesses), and the person-on-the-street interviews (in which, in an amusing inversion that also evokes an infomercial's staging of public curiosity, passersby pose questions of the camera, like "What *is* anorexia nervosa?" and "Do they really think they look attractive like that?") are as parodic yet informative as their counterparts in *The War Game*.

Haynes had experience in the public-television sector whose signature documentary styles he satirizes in *I'm Not There*. His *Dottie Gets Spanked* (1993) was funded by the Independent Television Service (ITVS), the creation of a 1988 congressional amendment to the Public Broadcasting Act.[30] As a direct result of its involvement with Haynes, ITVS came under fire for allegedly promoting an "anti-family agenda." One conservative critic told a congressional subcommittee that, in awarding public-broadcasting funds to Haynes, ITVS had effectively subsidized "a mockery of 1950s American family life from the producer of the cult homosexual films *Superstar* and *Poison*."[31] (The scourge of congressional Republicans and other conservatives, who bristled at Haynes's having been awarded a grant from the National Endowment for the Arts, *Poison* has been called "a big nail in the coffin of publicly financed art films.")[32] *Dottie Gets Spanked* was eventually broadcast on PBS stations, where it was often bookended by episodes of the documentary series *American Masters* (1986–), in which Scorsese's *No Direction Home* would be included. With its biographical profiles of prominent cultural producers, *American Masters* was a major influence on *I'm Not There*. (Kent Jones has suggested—convincingly—that the *Biography* franchise was as well.)[33] The distinctly televisual documentary on Christian Bale's character(s) is essentially a two-part affair, divided between a nostalgic summing-up of the folk revival of which Jack Rollins was such an integral (if enigmatic) part and a more investigatory, present-tense account of Pastor John, complete with a handheld (or shoulder-mounted) camera that circles and penetrates the premises of the Gateway Ministry, where the "onetime sixties folk hero," now "an active figure in the evangelical community," sits for an interview. (Greil Marcus says of this "film inside the film" that it is "a documentary made for evangelical TV," but Haynes claims that PBS, not Pentecostal television, was his inspiration; indeed, the style is largely that of *American Masters*, and the scope suggests far more than merely a commitment to the religious angle; the program's host says that Rollins has been silent for two decades, which would place the production in the mid-'80s.)[34] "Old things are passed away," Pastor John says in a response to a question about his personal history. "All things are made anew. It doesn't matter what I did before."

What follows is perhaps more observational—more suggestive of cinéma vérité—than a typical episode of *American Masters*. It departs from the reflective, historiographical mode, with its reliance on experts who act as talking heads, to offer a present-tense recording of one of Pastor John's performances—a concert that combines, and blurs the boundaries between, sermonizing and singing. "I've never lied to you," the pastor assures his congregants. ("You wouldn't doubt a man of the gospel," says Peckinpah's Cable Hogue in conversation with a banker. "Of course!" the banker cries. "That's the *first* man I'd doubt!") Pastor John, standing before a microphone on an elevated platform in a windowless recreation room, one hand on a wooden lectern and the other on his hip, addresses a few dozen followers, who stare up at him from their folding chairs. "What I didn't know," the pastor continues, "was that it didn't matter what kind of music you were playing: folk, pop, rock and roll—we're all rolled up in the devil's pocket, and I'm not talking about a devil with a pitchfork and horns. I'm talking about a spiritual devil, in the midnight hour, and he's got to be overcome, and we here in America, we *shall* overcome. What greater honor for a nation than to speak of God?" The pastor's sermon, with its assortment of quotations and a combinatory drive that brings together Pete Seeger (via Charles Albert Tindley) and Wilson Pickett, is an instance of Haynes's own commitment to pastiche, emblematic of the broader style of *I'm Not There* itself. But it also evokes a passage in *Chronicles*, in which Dylan recalls that Lyndon Johnson, as president, once "used the phrase 'We shall overcome' in a speech to the American people. 'We Shall Overcome' was the spiritual marching anthem of the civil rights movement. It had been the rallying cry for the oppressed for many years. Johnson interpreted the idea to suit himself."[35] One could say the same of Pastor John.

Even as he claims to have left the music industry behind, the artist formerly known as Jack Rollins cannot help but mine it for metaphors. His sermon is a kind of musical autobiography (the second-person address is clearly a proxy for self-reflection) that acquires both religious and nationalist attributes, collapsing God and country in a manner that prepares for a final, coercive statement on global politics. "For some say," Pastor John continues, "that the war to end all wars has already begun right now in the Middle East, where it is prophesized that the weak will fall, and that Jesus will set up his kingdom in Jerusalem. So why should we worry, when we're already free, right here and right now?" This, too, is an amalgam—a succinct expression of Christian Zionism, or the belief that the establishment of the state of Israel is not (just) a Jewish triumph but actually augurs the Second Coming of Jesus. (The pastor's lines derive from a speech that Dylan, fresh from Bible study at the Vineyard Fellowship in Tarzana,

California, delivered at a concert in the fall of 1979, when, as Andrew McCarron points out, he "openly preached to audiences with mini-sermons between songs," often citing *The Late Great Planet Earth*, the 1970 bestseller by Christian Zionist and Vineyard alumnus Hal Lindsey.)[36] It is also a useful prelude to the song "Pressing On," which the pastor proceeds to perform with a gospel choir and a few men on guitar, drums, piano, and keyboard. "Shake the dust off your feet, don't look back," the song begins, echoing the pastor's supportive description of the decisive return of Jews to the Holy Land. The stage is flanked by bulletin boards with various notices pinned to them. ("It looks like an AA meeting," Greil Marcus observes of the setting. "The people in the audience are human wreckage. But they are not an audience. They are part of the same fellowship that Pastor John is part of"—and "Pressing On" brings them to wide-eyed life.)[37] On one wall is a mural that appears to depict the conclusion of the story of the flood, from the Book of Genesis, with its symbols of sanctuary and renewal: dry land, a dove in triumphant flight, and "Noah's great rainbow" (to quote Dylan's "Desolation Row"). While Pastor John sings, children play by a table holding donuts and coffee.

No such "heterophonic religious community" can be found in *Eat the Document*.[38] That this rather jagged work would bypass television for the big screen was by no means inevitable, but rumors to that effect began circulating in print as early as March 1971.[39] *Eat the Document* was never officially released, though it ran for six weeks in the fall of 1998 at the Museum of Television & Radio in New York and Los Angeles—its first "theatrical" engagement since 1972. "No tour created as much controversy and artistic debate as Bob Dylan's 1966 tour of Europe," argued the museum's program notes. "Bombarded with shouts of 'Judas' and 'traitor' from his once loyal folkies, Dylan was transforming his music and himself with ferocious electricity. No longer was he the scruffy, socially relevant folk singer they idolized: his clothes were mod, his lyrics oblique, and the music loud. Dylan, the heir apparent to Woody Guthrie, had embraced rock 'n' roll." The museum described *Eat the Document* as a work of "enveloping madness" but also as "an extraordinary look into the artist's psyche." "Madly" resisting meaning, the film could nevertheless be understood as granting access to an identifiable "psyche"—or set of psyches. Anticipating Haynes's approach, the museum argued that "*Eat the Document* presents a multitude of Dylans to contemplate: weary and fatigued on tour; jamming with guitarist Robbie Robertson and country legend Johnny Cash; riding around with John Lennon; and confronting a dubious press and public." The museum even sought to reproduce the format—and experience—of network television, presenting *Eat the Document* with the periodic commercial interruptions for which Dylan's editing had (or so the museum claimed) dutifully prepared. "Because the program was turned down by ABC," the notes explained, "it has never been seen in its intended form. The Museum is now presenting the one-hour documentary with commercials from sponsors of *ABC Stage 67*, to show how the piece was originally conceived." This double exhumation—of *Eat the Document* and "vintage" TV commercials—reflected the museum's medium-specific mission, elevating ABC's authorship over Dylan's own even as it sought to exploit the latter.

The sponsor-driven "conception" and "intentions" that the Museum of Television & Radio cited were plainly the network's, not Dylan's. Indeed, it was entirely possible to present *Eat the Document* as a discrete documentary film, as the Whitney and the Academy of Music had demonstrated in the early

1970s, when they programmed it as such, without commercial interruption. By showing it with their own, carefully curated commercial insertions, however, archivists at the Museum of Television & Radio sought to suggest an epic clash between free expression and sponsor-specific messaging—between Dylan's aesthetic experimentation and ABC's perceived constraints. But Dylan was never going to subvert the commercial structure of American television. Unlike the Golden-Age anthology programs that it sought to replicate, each of which had been licensed by a single sponsor, *ABC Stage 67* was the product of an era of network television advertising in which only a tiny percentage of prime-time programming was actually licensed by advertisers. The shift from single to multiple sponsorship, which gave the networks greater power, made *Eat the Document* possible in the first place.

By centralizing ABC, programmers and other commentators could contribute to the myth of Dylan as heroically inscrutable and wholly resistant to the crass demands of commercial television. Promoting the museum screenings, *Los Angeles* magazine asserted that Dylan had simply "freaked out the suits at ABC."[40] His biographers have used strikingly similar language. One writes that *Eat the Document* "wound up being rejected by ABC for the plain reason that it was technically unsuited for broadcast, to say nothing of being far too incoherent to be shown as a TV documentary (as opposed to an art film, which is in the end what it is)."[41] Sounes says that ABC "would ultimately reject [*Eat the Document*] because it was believed it would be incomprehensible to a mainstream audience, indeed to almost any audience."[42] But no one from the network has ever corroborated such accounts.

The notion that *Eat the Document* was too extreme for network television is a myth as enduring as that surrounding

Dylan's 1965 Newport performance. David Hajdu notes of the
latter legend that it "has never borne scrutiny well." He sum-
marizes the story of Newport—a fable so powerful, indeed so
central to post-1945 popular culture, that Haynes could not
avoid retelling (and self-consciously embellishing) it in *I'm
Not There*: "having affronted his fans by 'going electric,' Dylan
was booed off the Newport stage, thrown from the temple for
propagating a new faith in rock and roll too radical for his
old followers to accept; humbled, teary-eyed, Dylan returned
to sing in his folk style, an act of contrition." "As a poetic allegory," Hajdu continues, "the story dramatizes the emergence of a new music through the union of folk and rock with
themes close to young people—generational conflict, style,
and rage."[43] Haynes highlights the mythic aspects of Newport
'65, framing it as a Felliniesque episode and drawing out the
combative implications of the legend that Hajdu and others
have debunked: in a kind of dream-within-a-dream—a "false"
or strictly metaphoric vision the more fantastical for its violent extremity—Quinn and his fellow musicians fire machine
guns at the crowd, in a frontal assault that also encompasses
the camera (and the film's viewer). Haynes prepares for this
moment as if for a hallucination (or a hit job). Quinn's limo
(which looks like a hearse) passes through a highway tunnel
in a sequence of shots patterned after *8½*. Appropriately portentous, this lead-up to Newport is scored to the increasingly
rapid beating of a heart. Two teenage girls, sharing the back
seat of their parents' car, silenced by the closed window, begin
clawing at the glass as soon as they catch a glimpse of Quinn
being chauffeured in a parallel lane. On the soundtrack,
Whishaw's Rimbaud speaks ominously of the musico-moral
state of things: "Woody Guthrie was dead. Little Richard was

becoming a preacher. So, whether you were a folk singer or a Christian, rock-and-roll was the devil." A close-up of Quinn's blood pressure being taken shows a typed draft of "Like a Rolling Stone" pinned beneath his forearm, a few words and phrases crossed out. "Me, I was in a ditch," the poet's narration continues, "up a cliff, out of step, ready to quit. I wrote the kind of stuff you write when you have no place to live and you're wrapped up in the fire pump." A brief shot of Rimbaud flicking the ash from his cigarette punctuates the muted scenes unfolding inside Quinn's limo, where Haynes's version of Albert Grossman (played by Canadian actor Mark Camacho) quarrels with another handler. The two men eventually train their anxious eyes on Quinn (and the camera) as Rimbaud's voice-over offers an extravagant confession: "I nearly killed myself with pity and despair. And then I wrote it." A fleeting image of Quinn seated at his typewriter precedes a slow overhead pan across the crowd assembling at Newport. Soon, Quinn is singing "Maggie's Farm" (1965), the very song that Dylan opened with at Newport '65. As Hajdu points out, this opener can hardly have shocked many of the music fans in attendance: "While some folk traditionalists in the Newport audience may have been startled to hear 'Maggie's Farm,' far more had been listening to it for months. . . . Nor could the sound of a group playing rock and roll on electrified instruments have come as much of a shock that evening," given that other acts, like the Paul Butterfield Blues Band and the Chambers Brothers, had already played their electric sets to much acclaim.[44] Yet "Maggie's Farm," whose refrain is an unambiguous refusal ("I ain't gonna work on Maggie's farm no more"), is very much a farewell—a repudiation—and that is precisely how Haynes employs it, with Stephen Malkmus's

The Newport myth.

singing voice (rather than an actual Dylan recording) coming out of Cate Blanchett.

Dylan may not have scandalized his Newport audience, but his later European tour, as depicted in *Eat the Document*, was anything but lovingly received. At L'Olympia in Paris, he performed in front of a massive American flag (which Haynes reproduces for one of Quinn's concerts, drawing attention to the performer's foreignness and also, possibly, his national chauvinism).[45] "This upset members of the French audience," writes Sounes, "partly because of America's controversial involvement in the former French colony of Vietnam. Bob seemed oblivious to the politics, as usual, even though his world tour coincided with a huge escalation in the conflict in Vietnam."[46] A similar obliviousness—or, perhaps, a deliberate obtuseness—was at work in Dylan's decision to name his mid-seventies concert tour after the apocalyptic US air war in Southeast Asia. Yet that, too, could be construed as a prototypically American tendency. As Richard Porton observed, "You get a sense from [*I'm Not There*] and the many biographies that even if [Dylan is] literally a liar he's connected to this bona fide and intrinsically American tradition of self-invention."[47] While preparing to make *I'm Not There*, Haynes had written in his notebook that the "governing concepts/themes" of the film would include the following: "America obsessed with authenticity / authenticity the perfect costume / America the land of masks, costumes, self-transformation, creativity is artificial, America's about false authenticity and creativity."[48] Subsequent debates about "cultural appropriation" have certainly complicated such matters. ("Authenticity was the rage in a folk scene dominated by white college kids and dropouts affecting the voices of the Delta," notes David Yaffe, emphasizing the persistence of racial impersonation, a kind of oral blackface.) Haynes's sense of the American carnivalesque does not ignore race (whatever the "colorblind" dimensions of Marcus Carl Franklin's casting), but it tends to suggest an uncritical, even naïve, embrace of national ideals that are plainly white-authored, and that would have been unavailable to, among others, a dark-skinned Black child hopping freights in rural America in the middle of the twentieth century.

SCORSESE CITES HAYNES

Viewed today, *Eat the Document* suggests the end of an era—the last time that it would be possible to publicly express antipathy toward Dylan without rousing his legions of defenders. Except for the occasional charge of plagiarism (leveled, typically, in a spirit of amusement at the artist's perceived effrontery in an age of digital surveillance and instant detection), the august Dylan is today exceedingly unlikely to experience hostility in any venue, something that makes *Eat the Document* seem even odder. Recognizing its distinctiveness, Haynes set out to "copy some of [its] constructions," as he put it. "What a crazy, irreverent, unorthodox approach to a rock doc that was," he continued. "There's no sense of organic continuity or living through a single performance. . . . It feels like it's driven by amphetamines or by a kind of restlessness, almost a refusal to ever be content."[49] For all its avant-garde trappings, and despite including the voices of a few supportive fans, Dylan's cut is unmistakably a record of the bile that he once generated as a public figure—of "the unabating controversy his music stirred everywhere."[50] Understood as a directive—a radical command—the film's title was, then, only partially realized. No amount of discontinuous editing could possibly efface the venom with which Dylan's performances were met throughout Europe in the spring of 1966. The film still *documents*, which is what made it such a useful source for both Scorsese's *No Direction Home* and Haynes's *I'm Not There*. Its historical subject wasn't fully consumed: future filmmakers could still imbibe it.

None of this is to say that Dylan, working in the field of film, did not produce stinkers after the off-putting *Eat the Document*. Edited down from some four hundred hours of footage, all of it shot during the 1975–76 Rolling Thunder Revue, Dylan's widely panned *Renaldo & Clara* features a plethora of musical performances but, as Pauline Kael noted in her scathing review, "keeps cutting away from the stage to cinéma vérité fantasies of Dylan's life, which occupy more than two-thirds of the movie." Kael continued: "Although the film was made by Bob Dylan, he didn't direct it (nobody did)."[51] "Bob envisaged the film," writes biographer Howard Sounes, "as much more than a concert documentary. It would be a work of art in the style of European auteurs, with Bob and his friends acting out dramatic scenes."[52] Dylan hired Sam Shepard to pen a script (of sorts) and told the playwright that François Truffaut's *Shoot the Piano Player* (1960) and Marcel Carné's *Children of Paradise* (1945) were among his inspirations.[53] (Dylan would also cite Peckinpah, Hitchcock, Godard, Warhol, Kurosawa, and Tod Browning as influences, and call Buñuel his favorite director.)[54] Four camera crews worked simultaneously on *Renaldo & Clara*, which also includes Dylan's own person-on-the-street interviews, conducted in Harlem, outside the Apollo Theater (whose marquee, visible in the background, is advertising Mark Robson's disaster film *Earthquake* [1974]). Dylan initially focuses on Black children, framed in a way that clearly influenced the opening-credit sequence of *I'm Not There*: in both instances (which also evoke Charles Burnett's portrait of Black children at play in his 1978 *Killer of Sheep*), Black kids congregating on a sidewalk look directly at the camera, challenging its infiltration of a public space that they have made their own. The kids in *Renaldo* are perhaps more playful than those in *I'm Not There*; the former mug for the camera and ask if their faces are going to appear on television, while the latter, silent while the soundtrack blasts Dylan's "Stuck Inside of Mobile with the Memphis Blues Again," appear resentful of the camera's presence as it glides past them in an elegant tracking shot. Eventually, the grownups take over in *Renaldo*, willing at last to acknowledge Dylan's persistent questions about Rubin Carter (he wants, he says, "to find someone who knows about him"). That they don't answer to Dylan's liking is indicated by his decision to silence the first respondent, whose mouth moves while a live performance of "Hurricane" plays over him. Indeed, such "interviews," as Kael observed, "seem included to show us that Bob Dylan cares more about black people than they do themselves."[55] Haynes's opening-credit sequence, featuring dozens of Montreal extras (and Montreal itself, its streets dressed as Greenwich Village), is not meant to be more than an expressionist montage showing various milieus that not only relate to Dylan's own provinces and referents (coffee houses, iron mines, Moondog) but that also, filmed in grainy black-and-white, mirror the preceding archival footage of the New York City subway. (That footage, showing various midcentury commuters, resonates with Scorsese's use of D. A. Pennebaker's debut film *Daybreak Express* [1953] in *No Direction Home*, which also quotes Dylan as saying of folk songs, "You could write them on the subway.") But Dylan, in *Renaldo*, invokes the penetrating promise of the documentary interview only to obliterate it with distracting and distortive audiovisual techniques that recall the dizzying, discordant *Eat the Document*. In the process, Dylan quite literally silences the speech of a Black subject and employs other strategies of alienation, all while purporting to demonstrate that even Americans of color—in Harlem, no less—require his "Hurricane" for its instructional value.

The influence of *Renaldo* is evident throughout *I'm Not There*. Haynes even offers a black-and-white variation on the earlier film's famous cemetery sequence, in which Dylan and Allen Ginsberg (billed as "The Father") visit Jack Kerouac's grave in Lowell, Massachusetts. The two men discuss the many other graves that they have seen (Hugo's, Baudelaire's, Keats's, Chekhov's) before Dylan announces, "I want to be buried in an unmarked grave." ("Of course," Kael wryly remarked of the utterance. "That's why he's made a four-hour movie about himself.")[56] In Haynes's version, Ginsberg and Jude Quinn, standing on a similar plot of land, stare up at a massive crucifix, mock it, and then dance a jig. (Ginsberg is frequently seen dancing in *Renaldo & Clara*, in which he also translates the francophone Stations of the Cross.) Dylan's film features various individuals who, as Kael put it, "playact identity games," swapping and multiplying personas in ways that seem to anticipate the playful transpositions of *I'm Not There*.[57] *Rolling Stone* reporter Larry "Ratso" Sloman (whom Joan Baez is said to have nicknamed for his resemblance to the Dustin Hoffman character in *Midnight Cowboy*) is repeatedly mistaken for Dylan; Sara Dylan enters a random building only to "become" Baez, who elsewhere dresses up like Bob and successfully passes as him; and so on. "There's Renaldo," Dylan told *Rolling Stone*, "there's a guy in whiteface singing on the stage and then there's Ronnie Hawkins playing Bob Dylan. Bob Dylan is listed in the credits as playing Renaldo, yet Ronnie Hawkins is listed as playing Bob Dylan."[58] Early in the film, Hawkins, as Dylan, encounters a reporter on a red carpet. "I want to know—are you somebody rather famous?" asks the reporter. "Bob Dylan," he answers. The reporter presses on, asking, "Would you like to tell me who Bob Dylan is—the true, real Bob Dylan?" Grinning triumphantly, Hawkins's Dylan declaims, "A hero of the highest order!"—to which the reporter can only ask, "Why do you say that about yourself?" Rather than offering his response, the film immediately cuts to him, in a different time and place, propositioning a young woman, telling her not to expect any kind of commitment from him, and inviting her to join his tour. Soon, the film shows Dylan himself driving an RV that serves as a sort of tour bus. Shots of the passing landscape, scored to a live version of Dylan's "I Want You," are re-created in *I'm Not There*, where they form part of a montage sequence featuring Claire and Robbie riding a motorcycle, with the very same song (albeit the original studio recording) on the soundtrack.

Dutifully promoting the film in 1978, Dylan said of *Renaldo & Clara*, "It's about the essence of man being alienated from himself and how, in order to free himself, to be reborn, he has to go outside himself."[59] In her review of the film, Kael went so far as to suggest that, contrary to legend, Dylan is, in fact, a unified personality, a man who, "despite his many guises, is always the same surly, mystic tease."[60] But if Dylan doesn't change, cultural expectations most certainly do. Kael argued that "what he does on the screen [in *Renaldo*] is painfully out of key with the times." She noted of his performance in the earlier *Dont Look Back* (of which, in her view, *Renaldo* represented a continuation) that he "was a put-on artist. He was derisive, and even sneering, but in the sixties that was felt to be a way of freaking out those who weren't worthy of being talked to straight. Implicit in the put-on was the idea that the Establishment was so fundamentally dishonest that dialogue with any of its representatives (roughly, anyone who wore a tie) was debased from the start."[61] Yet the concerts that *Renaldo* records were, by all accounts, appreciatively received. If *Eat the Document* offered evidence of the "war between musicians and their audiences"—waged throughout Dylan and the Hawks' 1966 tour of Europe—a chauffeur would describe the Rolling Thunder Revue as, by contrast, an ongoing "love affair between the performers and the audience."[62]

Renaldo & Clara premiered in New York and Los Angeles on Wednesday, January 25, 1978. A box-office disaster, it was quickly withdrawn. Yet it has had a curious, if "underground," staying power, as Haynes demonstrates in *I'm Not There*. (Like

Superstar, Renaldo & Clara has lived on largely in bootleg form.) In 2019, Netflix released Martin Scorsese's *Rolling Thunder Revue*, which purports to document the eponymous concert series. Scorsese necessarily draws on *Renaldo & Clara*, but he also utilizes "outtakes"—moments that Dylan's camera crews caught but that weren't included in the 1978 film. A series of "unplanned small gigs around the country," the Rolling Thunder Revue, which kicked off in Plymouth, Massachusetts, on October 30, 1975, was reportedly Dylan's attempt to recreate something of the intimate, improvisatory atmosphere of the Bleecker Street of 1961.[63] The tour unfolded in two parts: the first took place in the fall of 1975, the second in the spring of the following year. The last show of the 1975 fall tour, held at Madison Square Garden on December 8, was a benefit for Rubin Carter's legal defense fund. Dubbed "Night of the Hurricane," the fundraiser is, like Carter himself, featured in both *Renaldo* and the Scorsese film. Yet for all its reliance on *Renaldo*, the latter is deeply indebted to *I'm Not There*. Dylan may have threatened to thwart Scorsese's efforts to include him in 1978's *The Last Waltz* (in the end, Dylan, ostensibly worried that the Scorsese documentary would draw people away from his own, exactly contemporaneous *Renaldo*, permitted the use of just two of his live performances, along with the climactic group rendition of "I Shall Be Released"), but he has more than made up for such reluctance in the twenty-first century, giving Scorsese unprecedented access to his archives. Haynes, too, benefited from Dylan's new (if selective) largesse. But if *I'm Not There* borrows freely from *No Direction Home*, it is Scorsese who appears to be taking from Haynes in *Rolling Thunder Revue*, attempting, in particular, to approximate the latter's flair for mockumentary.

Scorsese fills *Rolling Thunder Revue* with clips and outtakes
from *Renaldo* as well as fake interviews and other simulations.
But he clearly lacks Haynes's camp appreciation of various
documentary styles. Nothing in *Rolling Thunder Revue* can
compare with the deliberately stilted person-on-the-street
interviews that Haynes contrived for *Superstar*—or, for that
matter, with Julianne Moore's mordant impersonation, in *I'm
Not There*, of Joan Baez's impossibly poised work as a talking
head in Scorsese's *No Direction Home*. A radiant Sharon Stone
gamely pretends that she once joined Dylan's revue; Michael
Murphy reprises his decades-old role as fictional politician
Jack Tanner; Jim Gianopulos, CEO of Paramount Pictures,
appears as a cynical tour promoter; and Bette Midler's hus-
band, Martin von Haselberg, plays the (fictional) filmmaker
said to be responsible for concert and "backstage" footage that
in fact derives from *Renaldo & Clara* (a rather uninspired attempt to deflect from that long-reviled project, which Scorsese
never identifies by name). These scripted interviews are neither expressive enough to distract and deceive nor awkward
enough to function effectively as parody. Scorsese aims for
the style that Haynes seems so effortlessly to achieve in films
as otherwise dissimilar as *Safe* (with its fake infomercials on
"environmental illness" and "chemical sensitivity") and *Poison* (with its uncanny mimicry of tabloid television). Haynes
is hardly alone in his repeated embrace of mockumentary, a
genre (or subgenre) that he certainly did not invent. But there
is a key difference between Haynes's mimicry of documentary
and Scorsese's, and it speaks to what Alexandra Juhasz has
described as mockumentary's capacity to "engage a subversive
or progressive project," namely by "underscor[ing] that documentary can be readily linked and unlinked to other cultural

and political projects that have contributed to injustice."[64] While Alisa Lebow, critiquing Juhasz's rather optimistic claim, rightly maintains that "subversion is simply not inherent in the project of faking," it would be difficult to deny that some mockumentaries are more productive—more resistant to mere nostalgia or self-satisfied cleverness—than others.[65] As Marcia Landy has suggested, the "quasi-documentary style" that Haynes employs in *Poison* "provides a critique of unreflective forms of non-fiction and the role of documentation."[66]

Nothing of the sort occurs in *Rolling Thunder Revue*, in which Scorsese's chums (Stone starred in his 1995 film *Casino*) simply indulge his vapid shuffling of "truth" and "fiction." In *Poison*, a (mock) television documentary, which concerns the disappearance of a Long Island boy said to have endured and inflicted all manner of abuse, is patently focused on the more salacious aspects of the case (such as the child's exposure to his mother's extramarital sexual encounter with a gardener). The gossipy, exploitative form of tabloid news, with its investigative energy and sham objectivity ("What *really* happened?" asks the documentary's voice-over narrator, echoing *Superstar*), effectively ignores larger questions about social power; race, class, gender, and sexual orientation are all occluded. Yet Haynes offers subtle invitations to read against the "innocent" grain of the television documentary, planting queer clues that yet (as in *Dottie Gets Spanked*, which also centers on a prepubescent child) resist recuperation by identity politics. (Seven-year-old Richie Beacon, with his mysterious penile discharge, can no more be fixed as gay than can *Poison* itself; the film also, of course, juxtaposes two other segments—"Homo" and "Horror"—that stand in dialogical relation to "Hero.") The mockumentaries woven into *Safe* similarly function as reminders of what commercially motivated "factual" media conceal, starting with their own economic self-interest. (They are commercial advertisements that masquerade as "scientific" public-service announcements; Haynes thus evokes the producers of *"actu-alité* television" who, in Klein's *Polly Maggoo*, foolishly insist that "quality programming adheres to norms untouched by the notion of profit," even as their state-run network struggles with punitive budget cuts, forced layoffs, and the desperate turn toward "salable" subjects like fashion models.) In *I'm Not There*, Haynes's parody of *American Masters*, which also includes elements of tabloid television familiar from *Poison*, begins with footage of Jack Rollins organizing Black voters (via the Student Nonviolent Coordinating Committee and "The Lonesome Death of Hattie Carroll") and ends by "exposing" his rebirth as Pastor John. It is—conspicuously—more concerned with "bring[ing] you face-to-face with the *real* Jack Rollins" (as its on-camera narrator so naïvely puts it), and with giving him an opportunity to further promulgate his brand of Christian Zionism, than with offering any insights into his social, political, or historical contexts. Haynes thus fashions both an imitation or a critique of Scorsese's own contribution to *American Masters*, which, like other entries in the PBS series, advances a cult of personality in the guise of historiography (or is it simply biography in the guise of public history?).

When Scorsese, in turn, pays tribute to *I'm Not There* in *Rolling Thunder Revue*, the result is a rather facile rendering of the by-now-axiomatic idea of documentary's unreliability. What's more, by mixing "fake" interviews with "authentic" ones (Scorsese conducted the former, Jeff Rosen the latter), *Rolling Thunder Revue* calls into question the recollections of histori-cal actors who are so rarely afforded the opportunity to speak for themselves, and who may not have consented to appear in what is, in part, a mockumentary. Ronee Blakley, who, as Pauline Kael complained, is so poorly served by Dylan's dialectical editing in the misogynistic *Renaldo & Clara*, tells Rosen about her time on tour.[67] (Rosen's interviews were conducted long before Scorsese's scripted conversations with Stone and the others, but their temporal and categoric difference is not marked—not directly registered or otherwise acknowledged—within the text.)[68] Seated in front of a piano on which rests sheet music as well as an official certificate noting her nomination for an Oscar for her performance in Robert Altman's *Nashville* (1975), Blakley offers an eloquent account of her experiences as a young performer. What is the purpose of impugning her by association with Stone's spurious reminiscences? Billed in the film's cheeky closing credits as "the ingénue," Blakley is absorbed into sophomoric metafiction. (Sharon Stone's saying that she was a childhood fan of the rock band Kiss and that she inspired Dylan to adopt some of their makeup routines, does not suffice as social commentary; it isn't even a good joke.) In contrast, *I'm Not There* suggests the complicity of documentary media in broader efforts to forget, downplay, or recast progressive political efforts. What, exactly, was the Student Nonviolent Coordinating Committee? What was its purpose? What obstacles did it face? What was its fate? Why did Black voters require organization in Mississippi in the summer of 1963? Such questions are routinely subsumed under curiosity regarding one man's "psychological" motivations and far-flung itineraries, as in the television program on Jack Rollins "becoming" Pastor John. Even *Dont Look Back* and the outré *Eat the Document*, as celebrity portraits, displace political history: in both documentaries, journalists question

Dylan's "commitment" to political causes without articulating the stakes of those causes. What would "sincerity"—Dylan's or anyone else's—achieve? What does its absence impede?

Scorsese opens *Rolling Thunder Revue* with archival footage of vendors in Lower Manhattan, all of them attempting to cash in on bicentennial fervor. One man is hawking handheld Confederate battle flags—an image that would seem to imply the persistence of racism and separatism within the bicentennial celebrations. But these stick flags serve as so many red herrings. Scorsese is not interested in interrogating race or class; like the journalists in the earlier documentaries, he frames such factors solely in terms of Dylan's "responsiveness" to them. He proceeds to offer a distinctly nostalgic account of the Rolling Thunder Revue, punctuated (like *Renaldo & Clara*) by Dylan's offstage encounters with adoring communities of color. (Borrowing liberally from *Renaldo*, Scorsese conveniently omits Dylan's condescending encounters with Black strangers on the streets of Harlem.) Rather than complicating the Nixonian glorification of the Carpenters, as *Superstar* so powerfully does, *Rolling Thunder Revue* seems simply to reproduce "official" affirmations of Americana in its extended, faux-naïve appreciation of the eponymous concert series. Scorsese might want to suggest that the Confederate battle flags visible in the found footage stand in ominous contrast to the seemingly equalitarian cheer of Dylan's revue, but they have long been central to the star's performances—iconically and affectively available in all manner of appearances. Even *Hearts of Fire* has Dylan joining forces with a musician who drapes himself in the Confederate battle flag; at one show, punks heckle them, and Dylan, as a defender of the old order, dives into the crowd to physically attack them.

Rolling Thunder Revue has Dylan once again playing a version of himself, but the film's simulations comment only on the genre of documentary rather than on the particular "truths" that it has purported to communicate or on the historical experiences that it has often helped to occlude. *Rolling Thunder Revue* offers Haynesian genre play without Haynes's queer critique. It is, of course, entirely possible that, rather than paying tribute to *I'm Not There*, Scorsese is in fact skewering the earlier film and, by extension, Bob Dylan's occasional cooptation by a queer theory seen as annoyingly inclusive and open-ended. But the idea of aged straight men "reclaiming" burlesque for themselves is even less appealing than the possibility that Scorsese's sensibilities are simply incompatible with the mockumentary's demands. *Rolling Thunder Revue*, which (toothlessly) mocks only aesthetic form, calls to mind Fredric Jameson's concept of "blank parody," by which Jameson means "mimicry without parody's ulterior motive, without the satirical impulse, without laughter."[69] What, exactly, if anything, is Scorsese ridiculing here? Has he a polemical intent? (And does he think that *these* jokes are funny?) "You have to know and understand something and then go past the vernacular," instructs Dylan in *Chronicles*.[70] It would be foolish to imply that Martin Scorsese lacks knowledge and understanding of documentary film. But it would be equally difficult to argue that he manages to "go past the vernacular" in *Rolling Thunder Revue*, which speaks merely the clichéd language of documentary's unreliability. As a sustained interrogation of Dylan's role(s) in cultural history, and a film that (to borrow Richard Dyer's definition of pastiche) "demonstrates that self-consciousness and emotional expression can co-exist," *I'm Not There* has yet to be surpassed.[71]

Playing On

Reviewing Norman Jewison's Rubin Carter biopic *The Hurricane* (1999), which makes repeated use of the eponymous Dylan song, and which, like *I'm Not There*, multiplies its subject into discrepant "selves" distinguished both formally (including via black-and-white cinematography that pastiches Scorsese's *Raging Bull* [1980], itself a pastiche of 1940s boxing films) and ideologically (Carter's competing "versions" include, in a particularly heavy-handed touch, whitey-hating devil and strictly victimized angel), Roger Ebert reflected on the matter of artistic license, writing, "Several people have told me dubiously that they heard the movie was 'fictionalized.' Well, of course it was. Those who seek the truth about a man from the film of his life might as well seek it from his loving grandmother. Most biopics, like most grandmothers, see the good in a man and demonize his enemies. They pass silently over his imprudent romances. In dramatizing his victories, they simplify them. . . . If they didn't, we wouldn't pay to see them."[1] (The film's credits include the disclaimer, "While this picture is based upon a true story, some characters have been composited or invented, and a number of incidents fictionalized." There follows an acknowledgment of Bob Dylan's production company, from which *The Hurricane* borrows footage of Dylan's Rolling Thunder Revue performing the title song in

Montreal.) Ebert's admonition could, of course, be used to explain the box-office failure of the intricate *I'm Not There*, which earned just over $11 million on a budget of nearly twice that. The split between domestic and international grosses favored the latter by far: the film earned only $4 million in rentals during its limited release in the United States—a poor showing even by the standards of an Oscar-oriented limited release—and more than $7.5 million in rentals overseas.

Echoing Ebert, critic Kent Jones, in a review of *I'm Not There*, suggested that anti-identitarian exercises simply don't sell—hence their relative scarcity in American cinema: "It doesn't take too much imagination to realize that this obsession with genuine articles and real things in American moviemaking is financial in origin: the general nervousness over budgets, percentages, and profits and losses is unconsciously transposed into dramas of identity hinging on disputed wills, water rights, marriage licenses or what have you. Celebrations of reinvention have come easily to poetry, fiction, music and dance but with much difficulty to the still costly art of moviemaking." Jones, who found *I'm Not There* "impressive"—a "ringing affirmation of the freedom to make yourself over"—implied that the film would be a tough sell at box offices, if only because of the abiding "dilemma of pastiche," which, he argued, requires a certain cultural fluency that the "mass audience" may not share.[2] (Indeed, *I'm Not There* had already bombed by the time Jones's review appeared in a December issue of *The Nation*.) Anthony Lane, who claimed that his "patience snapped" during the Gere/Billy sections, wrote of Haynes's citations, "Those in the know will feel smug; everyone else will be baffled." Lane's review concluded with a petulant, faux-populist question: "So who is this movie for?"[3]

More persuasive, and certainly more respectful of film audiences, is the faith that Haynes places in them. (In *Who Are You, Polly Maggoo?*, Grégoire announces, "I won't explain things. Let the viewer figure it out. No one explains things in real life. . . . Why explain things in a TV show? Even on TV, you can't talk down to the viewer. You mustn't explain anything, even for TV viewers, or you're bound to go wrong.") Dylan, too, has expressed confidence in the average consumer. In *Chronicles*, he describes a desire to challenge his listeners while trusting their meaning-making capacities: "That's okay, they could handle it," he writes.[4] In *Dont Look Back*, Dylan repeatedly insists to incredulous journalists that the young people who hear his "complicated" songs do, in fact, understand them. As Jeanne Hall points out, "Dylan is . . . consistently . . . contemptuous of reporters . . . who underestimate the intelligence . . . of his fans."[5]

If *I'm Not There* failed even to make back its budget, it was not necessarily because moviegoers "couldn't handle" Haynes's allusiveness. After its festival run in the fall of 2007, the film opened on 130 screens in North America. Its poor showing (it earned under a million dollars during its first, long weekend, which included the US Thanksgiving holiday) could not justify a wider opening in the new year. Neither, of course, could the film's sole Oscar nomination, which it eventually received on January 22, 2008—the day of Heath Ledger's shocking death. By the end of that month, the number of North American theaters showing *I'm Not There* had dropped to 39 from an all-time high of just 149. The film got a slight "Oscar bump" from exhibitors, who nearly doubled its number of screens for the first week in February. (The expansion may well have been a response not simply to Blanchett's Oscar nomination but also to Ledger's demise; both could reasonably have been expected to boost interest in the film.) By March, *I'm Not There* was playing in just 32 theaters in the North American market. It ended its domestic run (for American distributors, "domestic" grosses include Canada, where *I'm Not There* was shot) on March 6, 2008.[6]

Those who had been following the project's fortunes were not prepared for its box-office failure. *I'm Not There* had performed reasonably well with focus groups, even when its running time was still two and a half hours (a length to which the Weinstein Company strongly objected); at a test screening in New York in May 2007, the film's audience score was more than twice that of Haynes's *Far from Heaven*, which had been poorly received at a similar preview five years earlier.[7] Yet *Far from Heaven* would go on to earn over twice its budget; receiving four Oscar nominations, it was a modest art-house hit. *I'm Not There* would underperform it by nearly $10 million.

Despite the encouraging early screenings, Haynes and editor Jay Rabinowitz would feel compelled to whittle the film's running time down to 135 minutes. *I'm Not There* was the first of Haynes's features not to be edited by Jim Lyons, who died of AIDS-related illnesses while the project was in postproduction.[8] (The multitalented Lyons had been Haynes's lover and muse; *I'm Not There* is dedicated to him.) Premiering at the Venice Film Festival in the fall of 2007, *I'm Not There* received a ten-minute standing ovation.[9] The film fared nearly as well at the other major fall festivals, in Telluride, Toronto, and New York. Dylan continued to keep his distance. He declined to be interviewed for a *New York Times Magazine* article on the film, and he remained mum throughout its theatrical run.[10]

I'm Not There received mostly positive reviews and would

appear on multiple year-end top-ten lists. "After the Oscar 'legitimacy' of his ode to Douglas Sirk," wrote critic Kimberly Jones, "Haynes could've burrowed deeper underground or sold out entirely. Instead, he's created a dazzling hybrid."[11] Yet the film's box-office failure was difficult to ignore, and it raises questions about the salability of Haynes's central theme. *Carol* can be enjoyed for its apparent affirmation of lesbian identity; *Far from Heaven* for its similar critique of mid-twentieth-century repression; and even *Velvet Goldmine* for its celebration of glam rock.[12] *I'm Not There*, by contrast, is committedly anti-identitarian. Haynes sums up its theme: "Freedom from identity—that's really what, I think, Bob Dylan stands for and that's sort of what the ultimate message of the film is."[13] Whishaw's Rimbaud, quoting Joris-Karl Huysmans (by way of Bob Dylan), proudly declares, "I'm against nature." (Dylan's Jack Fate, in *Masked and Anonymous*, takes a somewhat different tack, observing, "They tell you that . . . the laws of nature are nonsense. . . . That's what they'd like you to believe.") Rimbaud's pronouncements are consistently enigmatic; they elude capture by identity categories—even minority ones. B. Ruby Rich famously described the style of the New Queer Cinema as "homo pomo."[14] While the "pomo" is abundantly evident in *I'm Not There*, the "homo" is not. And yet—structurally and formally, at least—*I'm Not There* is closest to *Poison*, that emblematic work of the New Queer Cinema, than to any other Haynes project. It doubles the earlier film's three interweaving stories and styles, retaining the use of mockumentary as well as the alternation of black-and-white sequences with ones shot and processed in color. In *I'm Not There*, as in *Poison* and perhaps especially *Far from Heaven*, Haynes re-creates both historical eras and some of the characteristic audiovisual forms and techniques of those eras. At the same time, he furthers his long-standing interest in visualizing a range of pre-cinematic landscapes: the early Americana of Riddle, where Gere's Billy the Kid roams, has precedents in *Assassins*.

Haynes's attempts to recuperate Dylan for queerness have usually been limited to libidinous descriptions of the star's androgyny as displayed in the mid-sixties, when, on a steady diet of amphetamines, he was at his thinnest. The sense of queerness as drag—a visible style rooted in specific sartorial choices—comes through in statements like "the Warhol Factory world . . . influenced how [Dylan] dressed and behaved," and "Even if you weren't in a totally queer world, you dressed and acted that way if you were going to be on the cutting edge."[15] "Male, white heterosexuality has been imposed on Dylan," Haynes once insisted, implausibly. To the filmmaker, the taunting tone of "Like a Rolling Stone" is "almost queeny."[16]

If the Butlerian notion that all gender is drag—that Dylan's subsequent expressions of "macho" were no less performed than his Warhol-inflected foppishness—comes into play here, the anti-identitarian crux of queer theory (at least as it was once understood) finds, perhaps, a deeper and more convincing expression in Haynes's defense of Dylan's inscrutability, a productive opacity that forms the subject (such as it is) of *I'm Not There*. Haynes, whose goal was to "challenge linear time and favor relativity," has emphasized the theme of "impersonation as freedom." He appreciates what he refers to as "the genuine weirdness of Dylan," as well as the signal audacity of his "passing as anything but the middle-class Jewish kid he actually was."[17] (Haynes, too, was once a middle-class Jewish kid.) Such an approach to queerness is more appealing, perhaps, than Haynes's gossipy claim that Dylan "had a total crush on Allen Ginsberg; they had a kind of love affair of the mind. And who knows what else?" Like David Bowie, Dylan has "said all sorts of provocative things about his sexuality"; for Haynes, their "veracity" is "less important than his instinct" to utter them.[18]

Opacity is, however, clearly an obstacle for some audiences—or, at least, for the marketing campaigns that seek to attract them. In his book on Haynes, Rob White reserves his harshest words for *I'm Not There*, which he calls "a high-production-values cover version that for the most part over-confidently misfires"; he identifies "something jaded" in the film, something blunted or perfunctory in its references to Haynes's earlier works.[19] White's dismissal may underestimate the appeal of Dylan's music, which suffuses the film's soundtrack and, for some, contributes to an exhilarating cinematic experience. Greil Marcus, who says that he "could hardly bear *Safe*" and that he has "almost never thought of" *Velvet Goldmine* since seeing it in 1998, loved *I'm Not There*. "It's immediately engaging," he wrote. "The film is confusing only if one demands that a dream explain itself—and if one refuses the implacable logic on which dreams float. When identity is as fluid as it is in *I'm Not There*—and when a person whose public life has been so bound up with the lives of other people wants to break the invisible contract between performer and audience—then the possibility must be present that identity can be cast aside altogether."[20] Marcus even defended the much-maligned Gere segment, writing, "Gere's performance—and the setting of a small country town where the citizens carry the names of characters in Dylan's crazy-quilt farrago of the mostly still-unreleased songs from the basement tapes—may be the key to the vitality of the film itself. . . . [Haynes] allow[s] the people of Riddle to step out of the basement and tell a story the real Dylan's songs never contemplated."[21] It is a story that defies description yet is so strange, so transfixing, so haunting that it is hardly surprising that critic Ed Howard compared it to David Lynch's *Mulholland Dr.* (2001).[22] "It's the Gere scenes, which have taken a critical shellacking, that are in many ways the most impressive, because they offer welcome evidence of Haynes's inventiveness," argued Kent Jones in his review of *I'm Not There.*[23] For Marcus, Haynes's "departure from the real is big enough for the reimagining or invention of moments that may go farther into Bob Dylan's real-life career than any writer, filmmaker, poet, or musician—any fan—has gone before." In Haynes's hands, the strange and distorted—the nameless and placeless—make a kind of "living sense."[24]

"I think it's a movie that will live on," Haynes has said of *I'm Not There*, "and I think it's a movie that really does respect its subject."[25] One way in which it has lived on is through its remarkable performers. In Jim Jarmusch's *Coffee and Cigarettes* (2003), released four years before *I'm Not There*, Cate Blanchett plays both herself and a fictional cousin; at one point in the film, the two even occupy the same frame, thanks to digital sleight of hand. The Jarmusch film suggests precisely the sort of fracturing and multiplication of a star persona that *I'm Not There* would take to even greater extremes. Even within Blanchett's own filmography, then, there was precedent for Haynes's approach to Dylan. But however much it may have drawn inspiration from Blanchett's previous work, *I'm Not There* has exerted an outsize influence on later stages of her illustrious career. The very same year she reteamed with Haynes for *Carol*, Blanchett appeared in *Manifesto* (2015), a 13-channel film installation written, produced, and directed by the German artist Julian Rosefeldt, who cited *I'm Not There* as the project's catalyst.[26] Upping the ante on her work in *Coffee and Cigarettes*, Blanchett plays over a dozen different roles in Rosefeldt's installation. More than merely a showcase for Blanchett's extreme versatility, the multi-channel *Manifesto* also mirrors *I'm Not There* in its cannibalization of various political and artistic movements and themes: each of the installation's thirteen segments boasts a voice-over narration that, delivered by Blanchett, quotes a particular historical declaration, whether Guillaume Apollinaire's "Futurist Anti-Tradition" (1913), Barnett Newman's "The Sublime Is Now" (1948), or Jarmusch's own "Golden Rules of Filmmaking" (2002). Much as she'd mouthed Dylanisms in *I'm Not There*, Blanchett in *Manifesto* would speak the words of legendary artists and intellectuals in an elaborate audiovisual collage. Many of Dylan's own inspirations communicate through her performances in Rosefeldt's installation. Also quoted are the filmmakers Dziga Vertov (born David Abelevich Kaufman), Stan Brakhage, Yvonne Rainer, Werner Herzog, Lars von Trier, and Thomas Vinterberg. There is even a direct echo of *I'm Not There* in the "Dada" segment of *Manifesto*, when Blanchett's figure, appearing at a funeral, chastises a crowd of mourners with words taken from the anti-establishment artist Tristan Tzara: "You are all idiots . . . made of the alcohol of purified sleep." (Compare Jude Quinn's response to a hostile audience in Haynes's re-creation of Dylan's 1965 performance at the Free Trade Hall in Manchester.) Even Blanchett's protagonist in *Tár* (Todd Field, 2022) recalls Quinn/Dylan. Born Linda Tarr in working-class Staten Island, she transforms herself into the world-renowned composer-conductor Lydia Tár, the new name announcing her temperamental identification with a wholly different milieu.

Other contributors to *I'm Not There* have similarly furthered their associations with Dylan. After his Oscar nomination for *The Messenger*, Oren Moverman cast Richard Gere in his 2014 film *Time Out of Mind*, whose title is taken from Dylan's oeuvre. The phrase, notes Sean Wilentz, is an old one, "long out of usage, meaning 'time immemorial.'"[27] Robert Siodmak's 1947 noir *Time Out of Mind* centers on a Maine composer who plagiarizes Debussy but whose theft is somehow inadequate: "I couldn't even steal it properly," he later confesses. "Of course, the notes are there. But it has none of his poetry, none of his soul. That's what makes a man's music his own." After three years in Paris, he returns in triumph, an "original" artist at last. (The film's narrator, a willful housekeeper in love with the musician, uses the eponymous phrase in voice-over to describe the period of his European exile, which so pained her that she can scarcely remember it.) For its part, Moverman's *Time Out of Mind*, in which Gere plays a houseless man living in New York City, evokes many of Dylan's own appropriated (plagiarized?) references to the down and out.

Haynes explains that he cast Gere because he wanted "an actor who carried with him a miniature history of American cinema." In other words, Gere's "own history on film [would be] part of [the] character [of Billy]. I wanted you to think about *Days of Heaven*—I wanted you to have flashbacks to [Gere's] earlier roles."[28] It isn't difficult to discern the connections between *I'm Not There* and Terrence Malick's 1978 film: near the beginning of *Days of Heaven*, Gere's character hops a freight train; like Billy the Kid, he's an outlaw, escaping first from Chicago and then, having killed again, from the Texas Panhandle, only to be hunted down and shot dead by the authorities.

The last Heath Ledger film to be released in the actor's lifetime, *I'm Not There* powerfully resonates with *The Imaginarium of Doctor Parnassus* (2009), the Terry Gilliam production on which Ledger was working at the time of his death. Rather than scrapping the project, Gilliam reconceived it along Haynesian lines. Ledger's sudden passing necessitated a strategy eerily similar to that of *I'm Not There*: three other actors—Johnny Depp, Jude Law, and Colin Farrell—would play three different versions of Ledger's character (and thus, of course, of Ledger himself), fleshing out the fantasy sequences that Ledger had not had a chance to shoot. The connections to *I'm Not There* are almost uncanny. Originally cast in the role of Robbie Clark in Haynes's film, Farrell had been forced, for personal reasons, to drop out before shooting began in the summer of 2006. Haynes, who had recently seen (and admired) Ang Lee's *Brokeback Mountain* (2005), promptly replaced him with Ledger.

Imaginarium evokes *I'm Not There* in other ways as well, including through its own citational tendencies. Many of the references are to Dylan and his milieus. Set in and around contemporary London, the film features a kind of traveling circus, which arrives, anachronistically, via horse-drawn wagon. Ledger's character, the roguish Tony, frequently wears a commedia dell'arte mask that recalls those donned by Dylan while on tour with the Rolling Thunder Revue (itself a kind of "imaginarium"). At one point, the actor Verne Troyer appears in blackface, recalling *Masked and Anonymous* and even *I'm Not There*. Depp's version of Tony speaks of Valentino, James Dean, and Princess Diana—all dead before their time—as being "forever young." "Don't worry if you don't understand it all immediately," counsels Christopher Plummer's title character, as if addressing the film's audience. Law's version of Tony tells Andrew Garfield's carnival barker, "Use your imagination!"

As in *I'm Not There*, Ledger here plays a celebrity attempting to outrun unwanted tabloid attention. "Don't believe what you read in the newspapers," he says, as the film skewers *The Sun* and *The Mirror*. Apart from his commedia mask, Tony is costumed in homage to Dirk Bogarde's von Aschenbach in Luchino Visconti's *Death in Venice* (1971), and this citational ensemble—white coat, white vest, white pants, white shoes—is multiplied across the different versions of Tony. (Gilliam also manages to insert a tribute to Georges Méliès.) Rather than offering a standard dedication, Gilliam signals the eccentricity of authorship: the film's closing credits begin with the words "A Film from Heath Ledger & Friends."

I'm Not There has also lived on in other tributes to Ledger. A decade after the film's release, Spike TV, a subsidiary of Viacom that has since been relaunched as the Paramount Network, debuted the documentary *I Am Heath Ledger* (2017). A feature-length production of Network Entertainment, the company behind the *I Am . . .* series of biographical films (which includes 2014's *I Am Steve McQueen* and 2015's *I Am Chris Farley*), the documentary, whose production was approved by the members of Ledger's family, opens with 8-millimeter footage of teenage Heath attending the Carnival of Venice, trying on commedia masks in eerie anticipation of *Imaginarium*. It is a measure of the lasting significance of *I'm Not There* that *I Am Heath Ledger* devotes so much time to it, offering clips along with original interviews with cinematographer Edward

Heath.

Lachman. Derik Murray, the founder of Network Entertainment, produced and directed *I Am Heath Ledger*, but he told the *Los Angeles Times* that, in his mind, the late actor had been his coworker in the endeavor.[29] Indeed, *I Am Heath Ledger* is premised on the idea that Ledger was, at heart, a director. (It consists largely of home-movie footage that he shot on various devices.) Eager to make a film on the life of Nick Drake, Ledger had chafed against the presumed limitations of the "traditional" biopic. "Heath," Haynes recalled, "was so kind of appalled by the prospect of a conventional biopic that he himself was turning [the Drake project] into something much more metaphoric."[30] In 2006, director and star discussed the very perils that they were then endeavoring to avoid or overcome with *I'm Not There*. Ledger apparently bristled in particular at what he perceived as the ethical transgression—the sheer effrontery—of purporting to speak on behalf of a historical subject, whether living or dead. Who, Ledger supposedly wanted to know, was he to "pin down" or otherwise "explain" the life story of another person? This, of course, is the crux of the question posed in the title of Dennis Bingham's book

Whose Lives Are They, Anyway?, which, fittingly, ends with a chapter on *I'm Not There*—"Some Conclusions on a Book Concerning Biopics" (a reference to Haynes's original subtitle, "Suppositions on a Film Concerning Dylan"). The dilemma, for Ledger, was, by all accounts, compounded by his own self-doubts. Indeed, the evident depth of his humility forms one of the themes of *I Am Heath Ledger*, in which the star is repeatedly described as unsure of himself, his insecurities out of all proportion to his talent.

"Maybe some documentaries should be love letters," Ben Harper said in praise of *I Am Heath Ledger*.[31] Whatever else it is, *I'm Not There* is a love letter to Bob Dylan, and to Ledger, too. The film is full of restless farewells. "Goodbye, my lady," Billy, at the close, calls out to his runaway dog, quoting the title of William A. Wellman's 1956 film—a "backwoods melodrama" about a stray Basenji answering to the name "Isis" (like the subject of Dylan's 1976 song), starring Sidney Poitier, Walter Brennan, and Brandon deWilde, who died in an automobile accident at the age of thirty. ("It's strange the way circles hook up with themselves," observes Dylan in *Chronicles*.)[32] Scored to the title song, Robbie's last appearance in *I'm Not There* is an exceedingly poignant one: after collecting legal documents from Claire—official papers that register the finalization of the divorce and custody arrangements—he simply drives away, slowly, jerkily, under a light rain. A reverse angle, shot through the car's rear windshield, shows a wistful Claire watching Robbie's departure, gracefully waving and blowing kisses, seemingly savoring her final glimpses of him before his car disappears down the road.

Acknowledgments

I think that I really fell in love with *I'm Not There* when I screened it in a course on queer cinema that I taught at Colgate University in the spring of 2013. The film wasn't even six years old, but it already felt indispensable. I remember sitting in the back of the theater, luxuriating in the music and in Haynes's audacity. I wept and felt exhilarated at the same time. I couldn't have asked for a better group of students, and I will always be grateful for my time at Colgate.

I want to thank passionate series editor Donna Kornhaber for her support, enthusiasm, and guidance, as well as for the inspiring model of her own scholarship. (The previous books in the series, including the brilliant volume by my friend and mentor Dana Polan, were catalyzing; they set the bar pretty high.) It was truly a pleasure to work with Donna. I am immensely grateful to her. I also want to thank the marvelous Jim Burr for his unflagging shepherding of the project, Mia Uribe Kozlovsky for her invaluable assistance, Lynne M. Ferguson for her expert editorial eye, and everyone else at the University of Texas Press for making this book possible. John Brenner provided top-notch copyediting, for which I am deeply thankful.

Nick Davis's eloquent, insightful manuscript report helped me to better understand my own arguments, as did the exacting work of an anonymous reader who alerted me to a few lacunae. I thank both readers for their careful attention to my work.

Dreaming of contributing to this exciting book series, I asked Joe Wlodarz what film to choose. He said, without hesitation, "*I'm Not There.*" As usual, he was absolutely right. His knowledge of Haynes's work is breathtaking, and his enthusiasm for it is infectious. He even managed to help me sort out the images reproduced in this book, and it was his long-out-of-print Canadian Blu-ray on which I relied. I'll never love *Velvet Goldmine* as much as Joe does, but then he'll never love *I'm Not There* as much as I do. We're even.

Notes

PROLOGUE. FLAMING QUOTATIONS

1. Rob Coley, "'I Don't Believe You . . . You're a Liar': The Fabulatory Function of Bob Dylan," in *Refractions of Bob Dylan: Cultural Appropriations of an American Icon*, ed. Eugen Banauch (Manchester, UK: Manchester University Press, 2015), 89.
2. Haynes, DVD commentary, *I'm Not There*.
3. John L. Geiger and Howard Suber, *Creativity and Copyright: Legal Essentials for Screenwriters and Creative Artists* (Oakland: University of California Press, 2019), 15.
4. Bob Dylan, *Chronicles: Volume 1* (New York: Simon & Schuster, 2004), 160, 196.
5. Dennis Bingham, *Whose Lives Are They Anyway? The Biopic as Contemporary Film Genre* (New Brunswick, NJ: Rutgers University Press, 2010), 26.
6. Jonathan Rosenbaum, "Allusion Profusion," in *Movies as Politics* (Berkeley: University of California Press, 1997), 171–178.
7. Denise Mann, *Hollywood Independents: The Postwar Talent Takeover* (Minneapolis: University of Minnesota Press, 2008), 248.

INTRODUCTION. 21ST-CENTURY BEDFELLOWS

1. David Yaffe, *Bob Dylan: Like a Complete Unknown* (New Haven, CT: Yale University Press, 2011), 46.
2. Robert Sullivan, "This Is Not a Bob Dylan Movie," *New York Times Magazine*, October 7, 2007, https://www.nytimes.com /2007/10/07/magazine/07Haynes.html.

3. Quoted in Jason Matloff, "Todd Haynes Takes on Bob Dylan," *MovieMaker*, November 18, 2007, https://www.moviemaker .com/im-not-there-todd-haynes-20080122/.

4. Dylan, *Chronicles*, 169.

5. Quoted in Oren Moverman, "Superstardust: Talking Glam with Todd Haynes," in *Velvet Goldmine: A Screenplay by Todd Haynes* (New York: Miramax Books, 1998), xv–xvi.

6. Quoted in Moverman, "Superstardust," xiii.

7. Quoted in Matloff, "Todd Haynes Takes on Bob Dylan."

8. Todd Haynes, "*I'm Not There*: Developing Dylan," in *A Killer Life: How an Independent Film Producer Survives Deals and Disasters in Hollywood and Beyond*, ed. Christine Vachon with Austin Bunn (Montclair, NJ: Limelight Editions, 2007), 194.

9. Peter Decherney, "One Law to Rule Them All: Copyright Goes Hollywood," in *Hollywood and the Law*, ed. Paul McDonald et al. (London: BFI, 2015), 23; Lyman Ray Patterson, *Copyright in Historical Perspective* (Nashville, TN: Vanderbilt University Press, 1968).

10. Haynes, "*I'm Not There*," 194.

11. Yaffe, *Bob Dylan*, 32.

12. Yaffe, *Bob Dylan*, 32.

13. Quoted in Matloff, "Todd Haynes Takes on Bob Dylan."

14. Vachon, *A Killer Life*, 198. Though not required by law, a life-rights agreement is a way of minimizing risk. "Obtaining consent in a life rights agreement from the subject person(s)," write Geiger and Suber, "certainly helps reduce the risk of litigation (frivolous or otherwise) and interference with production or distribution. Life rights agreements have become part of the required clearance package for biopics." Geiger and Suber, *Creativity and Copyright*, 33–34.

15. Phil M. Daly, "Along the Rialto," *Film Daily*, January 10, 1945, 9.

16. Matt Prigge, "It Ain't Me Babe," *Philadelphia Weekly*, November 21, 2007, in *Todd Haynes: Interviews*, ed. Julia Leyda (Jackson: University Press of Mississippi, 2014), 150,

emphasis added; Kim Wilkins, "'I Don't Know Who I Am Most of the Time': Constructed Identity in Todd Haynes' *I'm Not There*," *Film Criticism* 41, no. 1 (February 2017), https://quod.lib.umich.edu/f/fc/13761232.0041.103?view=text;rgn=main.

17. "Cal York's Gossip of Hollywood," *Photoplay*, November 1935, 42.

18. Geiger and Suber, *Creativity and Copyright*, 146. See also American Society of Composers, Authors and Publishers, "How to Acquire Music for Films," 2022, https://www.ascap.com/help/career-development/How-To-Acquire-Music-For-Films.

19. Yaffe, *Bob Dylan*, 55.

20. Eric Hoyt et al., "Introduction: On the Legal Lives of Hollywood," in *Hollywood and the Law*, 1.

21. Hoyt et al., "Introduction: On the Legal Lives of Hollywood," 13.

22. Mark Bartholomew and John Tehranian, "The Changing Landscape of Trademark Law in Tinseltown: From *Debbie Does Dallas* to *The Hangover*," in Hoyt et al., *Hollywood and the Law*, 62.

23. Quoted in Joshua Rothkopf, "Todd Haynes on 30 Years of New Queer Cinema: 'We Were Trying to Make Sense of an Incredibly Scary Time,'" *Entertainment Weekly*, June 30, 2022, https://ew.com/movies/todd-haynes-on-30-years-of-new-queer-cinema/.

24. Rob White, "Interview with Todd Haynes," in Rob White, *Todd Haynes* (Urbana: University of Illinois Press, 2013), 163.

25. *Rogers v. Grimaldi*, 875 F.2d 994 (2nd Cir. 1989).

26. Bartholomew and Tehranian, "The Changing Landscape of Trademark Law in Tinseltown," 54.

27. *E.S.S. Entm't 2000, Inc. v. Rock Star Videos, Inc.*, 547 F.3d 1095 (9th Cir. 2008); quoted in Bartholomew and Tehranian, "The Changing Landscape of Trademark Law in Tinseltown," 55.

28. Decherney, "One Law to Rule Them All," 25.

29. Decherney, "One Law to Rule Them All," 25.

30. Quoted in Geiger and Suber, *Creativity and Copyright*, 19.

31. For more on Gainsbourg's Claire and on the film's complex feminist reverberations, see Nick Davis, "Bringing It All Back Home, or Feminist Suppositions on a Film Concerning Dylan," in *Reframing Todd Haynes: Feminism's Indelible Mark*, ed. Theresa L. Geller and Julia Leyda (Durham, NC: Duke University Press, 2022), 299–316.

32. Yaffe, *Bob Dylan*, 48.

33. Geiger and Suber, *Creativity and Copyright*, 4.

34. Geiger and Suber, *Creativity and Copyright*, 14, 17, 22.

35. *Nichols v. Universal Pictures Corporation*, 45 F.2d 119 (2nd Cir. 1930).

36. Quoted in Anthony DeCurtis, *Lou Reed: A Life* (New York: Back Bay Books, 2017), 164.

37. Yaffe, *Bob Dylan*, 119.

38. Greil Marcus, "Old Songs in New Skins," in *Bob Dylan by Greil Marcus: Writings, 1968–2010* (New York: PublicAffairs, 2010), 234.

39. Jean-François Lyotard, "Defining the Postmodern," in *The Cultural Studies Reader*, 2nd ed., ed. Simon During (New York: Routledge, 1993), 143. For more on the film's relationship to postmodernism, see David Hanley, "Todd Haynes, *I'm Not There*, and the Postmodern Biopic," *Offscreen*, April 2016, https://offscreen.com/view/todd-haynes-im-not-there -and-the-postmodern-biopic.

40. Decherney, "One Law to Rule Them All," 34.

41. Peter Decherney, *Hollywood's Copyright Wars: From Edison to the Internet* (New York: Columbia University Press, 2012), 184.

42. Decherney, *Hollywood's Copyright Wars*, 84.

43. Quoted in Rothkopf, "Todd Haynes on 30 Years of New Queer Cinema."

44. Spencer Kornhaber, "Bob Dylan Cheats Again?," *Atlantic*, June 14, 2017, https://www.theatlantic.com/entertainment

/archive/2017/06/bob-dylan-nobel-spark-notes-plagarism /530283/.

45. Quoted in Yaffe, *Bob Dylan*, 93.

46. Sean Wilentz, *Bob Dylan in America* (New York: Anchor Books, 2011), 8, 12.

47. *Faulkner Literary Rights v. Sony Pictures Classics, Inc.*, 953 F.Supp. 2d 701 (N.D. Miss. 25 October 2012).

48. Matthew Belloni, "Judge: 'Deep Throat' Owners Can't Stop 'Lovelace' Release," *Hollywood Reporter*, August 7, 2013, https://www.hollywoodreporter.com/business/business -news/judge-deep-throat-owners-cant-602020/.

49. Justin Wyatt, *Poison* (Trowbridge: Flicks Books, 1998), 15.

PURSUING OPACITY

1. Anthony Scaduto, *Bob Dylan* (New York: Grosset & Dunlap, 1971), 18.

2. Quoted in Sullivan, "This Is Not a Bob Dylan Movie."

3. Quoted in Sullivan, "This Is Not a Bob Dylan Movie."

4. Jesse Schlotterbeck, "*I'm Not There*: Transcendent Thanatography," in *The Biopic in Contemporary Film Culture*, ed. Tom Brown and Belén Vidal (London: Routledge, 2013), 230.

5. Sullivan, "This Is Not a Bob Dylan Movie."

6. David Hajdu, *Positively 4th Street: The Lives and Times of Joan Baez, Bob Dylan, Mimi Baez Fariña, and Richard Fariña* (New York: Farrar, Straus and Giroux, 2001), 196.

7. Sullivan, "This Is Not a Bob Dylan Movie."

8. Sullivan, "This Is Not a Bob Dylan Movie."

9. Gene Maddaus, "Lionsgate Acquires Bulk of Weinstein Film Library in Spyglass Deal," *Variety*, July 15, 2021, https:// variety.com/2021/film/news/lionsgate-weinstein-co-library -spyglass-media-1235021200/.

10. Ethan Millman, "Bob Dylan Sells All Recorded Rights to Sony Music," *Rolling Stone*, January 24, 2022, https:// www.rollingstone.com/music/music-news/bob-dyan-sells -masters-sony-music-1289763/.

11. IMDb gives the title as *Bob Dylan's Home Movie*, but Dylan's biographers generally agree that the aborted project was too vague even for Dylan to title it. See, for instance, Howard Sounes, *Down the Highway: The Life of Bob Dylan* (New York: Grove Press, 2011), 224.

12. Jonathan Cott, "Bob Dylan as Filmmaker: 'I'm Sure of My Dream Self. I Live in My Dreams,'" *Rolling Stone*, January 26, 1978, https://www.rollingstone.com/music/music-news /bob-dylan-as-filmmaker-im-sure-of-my-dream-self-i-live-in -my-dreams-88435/.

13. Quoted in Yaffe, *Bob Dylan*, 37.

14. Roger Ebert, "*Masked and Anonymous*," in *Roger Ebert's Movie Yearbook 2006* (Kansas City, MO: Andrews McMeel Publishing, 2006), 433–434.

15. Sullivan, "This Is Not a Bob Dylan Movie."

16. Todd Haynes, DVD commentary, *I'm Not There*.

17. Vachon, *A Killer Life*, 200.

18. Sullivan, "This Is Not a Bob Dylan Movie."

19. Michael Denning, "Bob Dylan and Rolling Thunder," in *The Cambridge Companion to Bob Dylan*, ed. Kevin J. H. Dettmar (New York: Cambridge University Press, 2009), 34.

20. Sullivan, "This Is Not a Bob Dylan Movie."

21. Yaffe, *Bob Dylan*, 33.

22. Sullivan, "This Is Not a Bob Dylan Movie."

23. For more on suspect films, see Noah Tsika, *Screening the Police: Film and Law Enforcement in the United States* (New York: Oxford University Press, 2021).

24. Sullivan, "This Is Not a Bob Dylan Movie."

25. Haynes, DVD commentary, *I'm Not There*.

26. Haynes, DVD commentary, *I'm Not There*.

27. Sounes, *Down the Highway*, 240.

28. Ben Zimmer, "The Delights of Parsing the Beatles' Most Nonsensical Song," *Atlantic*, November 24, 2017, https:// www.theatlantic.com/entertainment/archive/2017/11/i-am -the-walrus-50-years-later/546698/.

29. Todd Haynes, quoted in Richard Porton, "The Many Faces of Bob Dylan: An Interview with Todd Haynes," *Cineaste* 33 (2007), in *Todd Haynes: Interviews*, 137.

30. Decherney, *Hollywood's Copyright Wars*, 73.

31. Woody Guthrie, *Roll on Columbia: The Columbia River Collection* (New York: Sing Out Publications, 1991); quoted in Will Kaufman, *Mapping Woody Guthrie* (Norman: University of Oklahoma Press, 2019), 58.

32. Sullivan, "This Is Not a Bob Dylan Movie."

33. Prigge, "It Ain't Me Babe," 149.

34. Todd Haynes and Christine Vachon, Blu-ray commentary, *Velvet Goldmine*.

35. Prigge, "It Ain't Me Babe," 149.

36. Prigge, "It Ain't Me Babe," 149.

37. Haynes, DVD commentary, *I'm Not There*.

38. Joan Hawkins, "Now Is the Time of the Assassins," in *The Cinema of Todd Haynes: All That Heaven Allows*, ed. James Morrison (London: Wallflower Press, 2007), 25.

39. Sullivan, "This Is Not a Bob Dylan Movie."

40. As Rob White points out, Haynes also evokes the *Screen Tests* in *Assassins*, another film in which an actor playing Rimbaud looks directly at the camera. White, *Todd Haynes*, 96–97.

41. Sullivan, "This Is Not a Bob Dylan Movie"; Jon Silberg, "Deconstructing Bob Dylan," *American Cinematographer* 88, no. 11 (November 2007): 41.

42. Quoted in Douglas Crimp, *"Our Kind of Movie": The Films of Andy Warhol* (Cambridge, MA: MIT Press, 2012), 8.

43. Paul Arthur, "No Longer Absolute: Portraiture in American Avant-Garde and Documentary Films of the Sixties," in *Rites of Realism: Essays on Corporeal Cinema*, ed. Ivone Margulies (Durham, NC: Duke University Press, 2003), 108. See also Noah Tsika, "'I Have My Choice': *Behind Every Good Man* (1967) and the Black Queer Subject in American Nontheatrical Film," in *Screening Race in American Nontheatrical Film*,

ed. Allyson Nadia Field and Marsha Gordon (Durham, NC: Duke University Press, 2019), 194–216.

44. Todd Haynes and Oren Moverman, *I'm Not There*, shooting script, quoted in Sullivan, "This Is Not a Bob Dylan Movie."

45. Haynes, DVD commentary, *I'm Not There*.

46. Sullivan, "This Is Not a Bob Dylan Movie."

47. Sullivan, "This Is Not a Bob Dylan Movie."

48. Steve Curwood, "An Afternoon with Pete Seeger," *Living on Earth*, April 17, 1998, https://www.loe.org/shows/segments.html?programID=98-P13-00016&segmentID=6.

VIOLATORS WON'T BE CITED

1. Pauline Kael, "What's Wrong with This Picture?," in *Movie Love: Complete Reviews, 1988–1991* (New York: Dutton, 1991), 12.

2. Sullivan, "This Is Not a Bob Dylan Movie."

3. White, *Todd Haynes*, 127; Sullivan, "This Is Not a Bob Dylan Movie."

4. Sullivan, "This Is Not a Bob Dylan Movie"; Nat Hentoff, "Bob Dylan: The *Playboy* Interview," *Playboy* (March 1966), in *Bob Dylan: The Essential Interviews*, ed. Jonathan Cott (New York: Wenner Books, 2007), 105; David Gates, "Dylan Revisited," *Newsweek*, October 6, 1997, in *Studio A: The Bob Dylan Reader*, ed. Benjamin Hedin (New York: W. W. Norton, 2004), 236.

5. Coley, "'I Don't Believe You . . . You're a Liar,'" 96n12.

6. Quoted in Sean O'Hagan, "Who Does Bob Think He Is?," *Guardian*, November 11, 2007, https://www.theguardian.com/music/2007/nov/11/1.

7. Sullivan, "This Is Not a Bob Dylan Movie."

8. Quoted in Emanuel Levy, *Gay Directors, Gay Films? Pedro Almodóvar, Terence Davies, Todd Haynes, Gus Van Sant, John Waters* (New York: Columbia University Press, 2015), 252.

9. Hawkins, "Now Is the Time of the Assassins," 26.

10. White, *Todd Haynes*, 77.

11. Eric Lott, "*Love and Theft*," in *The Cambridge Companion to Bob Dylan*, 172.

12. In White, "Interview with Todd Haynes," 159.

13. Geiger and Suber, *Creativity and Copyright*, 30.

14. Decherney, *Hollywood's Copyright Wars*, 60.

15. Quoted in Greil Marcus, "Bob Dylan Times Six: An Interview with 'I'm Not There' Director Todd Haynes," *Rolling Stone*, November 29, 2007, https://www.rollingstone.com/tv-movies/tv-movie-news/bob-dylan-times-six-an-interview-with-im-not-there-director-todd-haynes-67251/.

16. Sullivan, "This Is Not a Bob Dylan Movie."

17. Michael Phillips, "For 'Carol,' Director Todd Haynes Dug Deep," *Chicago Tribune*, December 17, 2015, https://www.chicagotribune.com/entertainment/movies/ct-todd-haynes-mov-1218-20151217-column.html.

18. Phillips, "For 'Carol,' Director Todd Haynes Dug Deep."

19. Patricia White, "Lesbian Reverie: *Carol* in History and Fantasy," in *Reframing Todd Haynes*, 39.

20. Geiger and Suber, *Creativity and Copyright*, 17.

21. Yaffe, *Bob Dylan*, 99.

22. Yaffe, *Bob Dylan*, 99.

23. Marcus, "*I'm Not There*," in *Bob Dylan by Greil Marcus*, 375.

24. David Yaffe, *Reckless Daughter: A Portrait of Joni Mitchell* (New York: Sarah Crichton Books, 2017), 199–201.

25. Greil Marcus, "Logical Conclusions," in *Bob Dylan by Greil Marcus*, 99–100.

26. Hawkins, "Now Is the Time of the Assassins," 30.

27. White, *Todd Haynes*, 2.

28. Jonathan Kahana, *Intelligence Work: The Politics of American Documentary* (New York: Columbia University Press, 2008), 7.

29. White, *Todd Haynes*, 2.

30. White, "Lesbian Reverie," 33.

31. Todd Haynes, "Three Screenplays: An Introduction," in Todd Haynes, *Far from Heaven, Safe, and Superstar: Three Screenplays* (New York: Grove Press, 2003), vii–xii.

32. Haynes, "*I'm Not There*," 195.

33. Yaffe, *Bob Dylan*, 24, 27.

34. Haynes and Vachon, Blu-ray commentary, *Velvet Goldmine*.

35. Dylan, *Chronicles*, 146–147.

36. Yaffe, *Bob Dylan*, 34.

37. Sullivan, "This Is Not a Bob Dylan Movie."

38. Quoted in Silberg, "Deconstructing Bob Dylan," 41.

39. Silberg, "Deconstructing Bob Dylan," 43–48.

40. Scott MacDonald, "From Underground to Multiplex: An Interview with Todd Haynes," *Film Quarterly* 62, no. 3 (Spring 2009): 54–64; in *Todd Haynes Interviews*, 168.

41. The scanning of the negative, however, was done without any grain suppression. Silberg, "Deconstructing Bob Dylan," 40, 48, 51.

42. Dylan, *Chronicles*, 113.

43. Quoted in Yaffe, *Bob Dylan*, 69.

44. Yaffe, *Bob Dylan*, 17.

45. For more on Haynes's affection for Pakula's work, see Rothkopf, "Todd Haynes on 30 Years of New Queer Cinema."

46. Anthony Lane, "Tangled Up," *New Yorker*, November 18, 2007, https://www.newyorker.com/magazine/2007/11/26/tangled-up.

47. Sean Latham, "Songwriting," in *The World of Bob Dylan*, ed. Sean Latham (New York: Cambridge University Press, 2021), 36.

48. Samuel Moyn, *Humane: How the United States Abandoned Peace and Reinvented War* (New York: Farrar, Straus and Giroux, 2021), 170.

49. Joan Baez, *And a Voice to Sing With: My Story* (New York: Summit Books, 1987), 199.

50. Sullivan, "This Is Not a Bob Dylan Movie."

51. Yaffe, *Bob Dylan*, 101.

52. *Damiano v. Sony Music Entertainment, Inc.*, 975 F. Supp. 623 (D.N.J. 1997).

53. Lee Glendinning, "Dylan Issues Legal Action over Biopic of Edie Sedgwick," *Independent*, December 15, 2006, https://www.independent.co.uk/arts-entertainment/music/news

/dylan-issues-legal-action-over-biopic-of-edie-sedgwick
-428588.html.

54. Adrien Brody certainly would have worked in this respect, and he was originally cast in *I'm Not There*, but he was forced to pull out when the project dragged on without adequate financing. Brody was to play Jack Rollins. Sullivan, "This Is Not a Bob Dylan Movie"; Vachon, *A Killer Life*, 200. Haynes has said that Brody was his first choice to play Rollins, "but he was sort of hemming and hawing." Quoted in Matloff, "Todd Haynes Takes on Bob Dylan."

55. Jada Yuan, "The Freewheelin' Hayden," *New York*, February 2, 2007, https://nymag.com/news/intelligencer/27368/.

56. Yuan, "The Freewheelin' Hayden."

57. Quoted in Glendinning, "Dylan Issues Legal Action."

58. Wilentz, *Bob Dylan in America*, 279.

59. Dylan, *Chronicles*, 35.

60. Michael DeAngelis, "There and 'Not There': Todd Haynes and the Queering of Genre," *Celebrity Studies* 8, no. 3 (2017): 585.

61. "I Am My Words," *Newsweek*, November 4, 1963, 94.

62. Quoted in Hajdu, *Positively 4th Street*, 194.

63. The handwritten paper, for which Zimmerman received an A minus, was exhibited at the University of Minnesota in the spring of 2006. David Pichaske, *Song of the North Country: A Midwest Framework to the Songs of Bob Dylan* (New York: Continuum, 2010), 217.

64. Wilentz, *Bob Dylan in America*, 299.

65. Wilentz, *Bob Dylan in America*, 299.

66. Phyllis Schlafly, "Fads and Follies in Public Schools," *The Phyllis Schlafly Report*, March 2003, https://eagleforum.org /psr/2003/mar03/psrmar03.shtml.

67. Sounes, *Down the Highway*, 454.

68. Motoko Rich, "Who's This Guy Dylan Who's Borrowing Lines from Henry Timrod?," *New York Times*, September 14, 2006, https://www.nytimes.com/2006/09/14/arts/music /14dyla.html?ref=books.

69. Kimberly Jones, "*I'm Not There*," *Austin Chronicle*, November 23, 2007, https://www.austinchronicle.com/events/film/2007-11-21/im-not-there/.
70. Yaffe, *Bob Dylan*, 60.
71. Haynes, DVD commentary, *I'm Not There*.
72. Dylan, *Chronicles*, 31.
73. Dylan, *Chronicles*, 20.
74. Marcus, "*I'm Not There*," 371.
75. Haynes, DVD commentary, *I'm Not There*.
76. Leland Poague, *Another Frank Capra* (New York: Cambridge University Press, 1994), 10.
77. Earl Hobson Smith, *Stephen Foster; Or, Weep No More My Lady: A Biographical Play on the Life of Stephen Collins Foster, Father of American Folk Songs* (Knoxville, TN: The Foster Players, 1926).
78. Bob Dylan, *Tarantula* (New York: St. Martin's Press, [1971] 1994), 101.
79. Yaffe, *Reckless Daughter*, 76.
80. Yaffe, *Reckless Daughter*, 76.
81. Eugen Banauch, "Refractions of Bob Dylan: An Introduction," in *Refractions of Bob Dylan*, 4–5.
82. Quoted in Danielle Paquette, "Bob Dylan: 'Wussies and Pussies' Complain About Plagiarism," *The Wrap*, September 12, 2012, https://www.thewrap.com/wussies-and-pussies-complain-about-plagiarism-says-bob-dylan-new-interview-56181/.
83. Quoted in Porton, "The Many Faces of Bob Dylan," 133.
84. Michael Gray, "'Rearrange Their Faces and Give Them All Another Name': On Bob Dylan and *I'm Not There*," *Sight and Sound*, May 21, 2021, https://www.bfi.org.uk/sight-and-sound/features/im-not-there-todd-haynes-homage-bob-dylan.
85. Porton, "The Many Faces of Bob Dylan," 133.
86. Stephen Scobie, "Plagiarism, Bob, Jean-Luc and Me," in *Refractions of Bob Dylan*, 198.
87. Quoted in Porton, "The Many Faces of Bob Dylan," 136.

88. Marcus, *"I'm Not There,"* 372.

89. Gray, "'Rearrange Their Faces and Give Them All Another Name.'"

90. Yaffe, *Bob Dylan*, 9–10, 32. Later, Yaffe is more equivocal, writing of "Like a Rolling Stone," "The song explodes with fury, but it's never been clear exactly who its target is. Speculations have ranged from Edie Sedgwick in particular to his audience in general, with more than a modicum of misogyny in the former case, misanthropy in the latter" (72).

91. Quoted in *"Factory Girl* Defaming Dylan?," *Stereogum*, December 14, 2006.

92. Sullivan, "This Is Not a Bob Dylan Movie."

93. Hajdu, *Positively 4th Street*, 120–121.

94. George Hickenlooper, DVD commentary, *Factory Girl*.

95. Hickenlooper, DVD commentary, *Factory Girl*.

96. Haynes, *"I'm Not There,"* 195.

97. For a dissenting (and musicological) view of this much-maligned segment, see Jacob Smith, "A Town Called Riddle: Excavating Todd Haynes's *I'm Not There," Screen* 51, no. 1 (Spring 2010): 71–78.

98. Sullivan, "This Is Not a Bob Dylan Movie."

99. Thomas Doherty, *Hollywood's Censor: Joseph I. Breen and the Production Code Administration* (New York: Columbia University Press, 2007), 339.

100. "Cate Blanchett on Cannes 2018, Harvey Weinstein & 'Carol,' and a Harmonica Solo," *Variety*, May 2, 2018, https://www.youtube.com/watch?v=FdY9WQ3ppEc.

MOCK THE DOCUMENTARY

1. There is, however, a shot of a newspaper article that says of Roberts that "he may become another Bob Dylan." But the print is small, and the shot itself is held for barely a second; pausing the image is the only way to really see Dylan's name. What the prediction means, in the film's terms, is unclear. Will Roberts "become another Bob Dylan" by shedding his apparent political commitments? Or is the suggestion rather

that Dylan was reactionary all along—that Roberts's musical appropriations are less perversions than extensions of *The Freewheelin' Bob Dylan* and *The Times They Are a-Changin'*?

2. Kahana, *Intelligence Work*, 150.

3. Haynes, "*I'm Not There*," 193.

4. Quoted in Yaffe, *Bob Dylan*, 90.

5. Quoted in Yaffe, *Bob Dylan*, 91.

6. Tim Grierson, "Tim Robbins Is Asking You to Pirate 'Bob Roberts' Before the Election," *MEL Magazine*, October 12, 2020, https://melmagazine.com/en-us/story/tim-robbins -interview-bob-roberts-movie-download.

7. Pauline Kael, "The Calvary Gig," in *When the Lights Go Down* (New York: Holt, Rinehart and Winston, 1980), 400.

8. Quoted in Grierson, "Tim Robbins Is Asking You to Pirate 'Bob Roberts' Before the Election."

9. Wilentz, *Bob Dylan in America*, 158.

10. "Not Seen in 20 Years: Bob Dylan's *Eat the Document*," Museum of Television & Radio handbill, Fall 1998.

11. William Boddy, *Fifties Television: The Industry and Its Critics* (Urbana: University of Illinois Press, 1990; repr., 1993), 144, 187–188.

12. "Activities of Regulatory and Enforcement Agencies Relating to Small Business," May 12, 1966, House of Representatives, Subcommittee No. 6, in *Activities of Regulatory and Enforcement Agencies Relating to Small Business: Hearings Before Subcommittee No. 6 of the Select Committee on Small Business, House of Representatives, Eighty-Ninth Congress, Second Session* (Washington, DC: Government Printing Office, 1966), 587.

13. Boddy, *Fifties Television*.

14. Boddy, *Fifties Television*, 164.

15. "Activities of Regulatory and Enforcement Agencies Relating to Small Business," 593.

16. Sounes, *Down the Highway*, 213.

17. Sounes, *Down the Highway*, 219–220.

18. Sounes, *Down the Highway*, 223; Greil Marcus, *The Old,*

Weird America: The World of Bob Dylan's Basement Tapes (New York: Picador, 2011), 231.

19. Quoted in Sounes, *Down the Highway*, 213.
20. "Not Seen in 20 Years."
21. Marcus, "Bob Dylan Times Six."
22. Seth Rogovoy, *Bob Dylan: Prophet, Mystic, Poet* (New York: Scribner, 2009), 105.
23. Sounes, *Down the Highway*, 213.
24. Sounes, *Down the Highway*, 213.
25. Marcus, *The Old, Weird America*, 231.
26. Kahana, *Intelligence Work*, 212, 166.
27. Kahana, *Intelligence Work*, 167.
28. Quoted in Porton, "The Many Faces of Bob Dylan," 132.
29. Haynes, "*I'm Not There*," 195.
30. John Thornton Caldwell, "Independent Television Service," in *The Encyclopedia of Television*, vol. 1, ed. Horace Newcomb (New York: Fitzroy Dearborn, 2nd ed., 2004), 1172–1173.
31. Testimony of Robert H. Knight, Director of Cultural Studies, Family Research Council, January 19, 1995, Corporation for Public Broadcasting, Fiscal 1996 Appropriation, House Appropriations, Subcommittee on Labor, Health and Education, in *Downsizing Government and Setting Priorities of Federal Programs: Hearings Before Subcommittees of the Committee on Appropriations, House of Representatives, One Hundred Fourth Congress, First Session* (Washington, DC: Government Printing Office, 1995), 964.
32. Sullivan, "This Is Not a Bob Dylan Movie."
33. Kent Jones, "Chaos, Clocks, Juxtapositions," *Nation*, December 6, 2007, https://www.thenation.com/article/archive/chaos-clocks-juxtapositions/.
34. Marcus, "*I'm Not There*," 374.
35. Dylan, *Chronicles*, 90.
36. Andrew McCarron, "Christianity: An Exegesis of *Modern Times*," in *The World of Bob Dylan*, 229; Wilentz, *Bob Dylan in America*, 177.

37. Marcus, "*I'm Not There*," 374–375.

38. Wilfrid Mellers, *A Darker Shade of Pale: A Backdrop to Bob Dylan* (London: Faber and Faber, 1984), 43; quoted in Denning, "Bob Dylan and Rolling Thunder," 38.

39. John R. Packer & Mellette, "DISCourse," *Hollywood Studio Magazine*, March 1971, 14.

40. "Bob Dylan's *Eat the Document*, Through Nov. 22," *Los Angeles*, November 1998, 139.

41. Rogovoy, *Bob Dylan*, 105–106.

42. Sounes, *Down the Highway*, 218.

43. Hajdu, *Positively 4th Street*, 259.

44. Hajdu, *Positively 4th Street*, 259–260.

45. "We cannot decide on the meaning of Dylan's gesture to sing in front of this national symbol," caution Carolyn D'Cruz and Glenn D'Cruz, "any more than we can arrest the meaning of the American flag once and for all." Carolyn D'Cruz and Glenn D'Cruz, "'Even the Ghost Was More than One Person': Hauntology and Authenticity in Todd Haynes's *I'm Not There*," *Film-Philosophy* 17, no. 1 (2013): 317.

46. Sounes, *Down the Highway*, 216.

47. Porton, "The Many Faces of Bob Dylan," 135.

48. Sullivan, "This Is Not a Bob Dylan Movie."

49. Marcus, "Bob Dylan Times Six."

50. Hajdu, *Positively 4th Street*, 281.

51. Kael, "The Calvary Gig," 397. Dylan himself broke it down thus: "About a third is improvised, about a third is determined, and about a third is blind luck." Quoted in Cott, "Bob Dylan as Filmmaker."

52. Sounes, *Down the Highway*, 294.

53. Sounes, *Down the Highway*, 294; Wilentz, *Bob Dylan in America*, 160.

54. Cott, "Bob Dylan as Filmmaker."

55. Kael, "The Calvary Gig," 400.

56. Kael, "The Calvary Gig," 401.

57. Kael, "The Calvary Gig," 399.

58. Cott, "Bob Dylan as Filmmaker."

59. Quoted in Sounes, *Down the Highway*, 314.

60. Kael, "The Calvary Gig," 397.

61. Kael, "The Calvary Gig," 398.

62. Footage of the chauffeur is included in Scorsese's *Rolling Thunder Revue*.

63. Yaffe, *Reckless Daughter*, 199; Denning, "Bob Dylan and Rolling Thunder."

64. Alexandra Juhasz and Jesse Lerner, "Phony Definitions and Troubling Taxonomies of the Fake Documentary," in *F Is for Phony: Fake Documentary and Truth's Undoing*, ed. Alexandra Juhasz and Jesse Lerner (Minneapolis: University of Minnesota Press, 2006), 5.

65. Alisa Lebow, "Faking What? Making a Mockery of Documentary," in *F Is for Phony*, 224.

66. Marcia Landy, "Storytelling and Information in Todd Haynes' Films," in *The Cinema of Todd Haynes*, 13.

67. Kael, "The Calvary Gig," 400.

68. See Chris Willman, "Ronee Blakley Remembers Bob Dylan's Rolling Thunder Revue: 'We Were Delirious,'" *Variety*, June 14, 2019, https://variety.com/2019/music/news/ronee -blakley-interview-rolling-thunder-revue-1203243802/

69. Fredric Jameson, "Postmodernism and Consumer Society," in *The Anti-Aesthetic: Essays on Postmodern Culture*, ed. Hal Foster (Port Townsend, WA: Bay Press, 1983), 114.

70. Dylan, *Chronicles*, 51.

71. Richard Dyer, *Pastiche* (New York: Routledge, 2007), 4.

PLAYING ON

1. Roger Ebert, "*The Hurricane*," *Chicago Sun-Times*, January 7, 2000, https://www.rogerebert.com/reviews/the-hurricane -2000.

2. Jones, "Chaos, Clocks, Juxtapositions."

3. Lane, "Tangled Up."

4. Dylan, *Chronicles*, 161.

5. Jeanne Hall, "'Don't You Ever Just Watch?' American Cinema Verité and *Dont Look Back*," in *Documenting the*

Documentary: Close Readings of Documentary Film and Video, ed. Barry Keith Grant and Jeannette Sloniowski (Detroit: Wayne State University Press, 1998), 228.

6. All figures are taken from Box Office Mojo, https://www.boxofficemojo.com/release/rl1331398145/.

7. Sullivan, "This Is Not a Bob Dylan Movie."

8. Sullivan, "This Is Not a Bob Dylan Movie."

9. Sullivan, "This Is Not a Bob Dylan Movie."

10. Sullivan, "This Is Not a Bob Dylan Movie."

11. Jones, "*I'm Not There.*"

12. This is not to say that such enjoyment is always complete or uncomplicated. In an important essay on *Carol*, Patricia White wisely cautions against underestimating the film's complexity and notes that the ending, in which separated lovers are finally reunited, is not necessarily—or not simply—happy. White, "Lesbian Reverie," 44. White's take on *Carol*'s ending echoes Greil Marcus's account of the concluding moments of *I'm Not There*. Marcus writes that "you don't know what really happens in Riddle, or, if Billy does escape, where he could possibly go. And that is why, leaving the theater, you are already on your way back in." Marcus, "*I'm Not There*," 376.

13. Haynes, DVD commentary, *I'm Not There*.

14. B. Ruby Rich, *New Queer Cinema: The Director's Cut* (Durham, NC: Duke University Press, 2013), 18.

15. Quoted in Porton, "The Many Faces of Bob Dylan," 132.

16. Quoted in O'Hagan, "Who Does Bob Think He Is?"

17. Haynes, DVD commentary, *I'm Not There*.

18. Quoted in Porton, "The Many Faces of Bob Dylan," 132.

19. White, *Todd Haynes*, 94–95.

20. Marcus, "*I'm Not There*," 370, 375.

21. Marcus, "*I'm Not There*," 373.

22. In Jason Bellamy and Ed Howard, "The Conversations: Todd Haynes," *Slant Magazine*, August 16, 2010, https://www.slantmagazine.com/film/the-conversations-todd-haynes/.

23. Jones, "Chaos, Clocks, Juxtapositions."

24. Marcus, "*I'm Not There*," 374.

25. Haynes, DVD commentary, *I'm Not There*.

26. Stephanie Bunbury, "Cate Blanchett as You've Never Seen Her Before," *Sydney Morning Herald*, November 11, 2015, https://www.smh.com.au/entertainment/cate-blanchett-as -youve-never-seen-her-before-20151110-gkuwmu.html.

27. Wilentz, *Bob Dylan in America*, 256–257.

28. Haynes, DVD commentary, *I'm Not There*.

29. Joe Donnelly, "Perspective: Heath Ledger's Sister Says It Took Blessing from Michelle Williams to Get New Documentary Made," *Los Angeles Times*, May 23, 2017, https://www.latimes .com/entertainment/la-et-st-i-am-heath-ledger-spike-tv -20170520-htmlstory.html.

30. Quoted in Matloff, "Todd Haynes Takes on Bob Dylan."

31. Quoted in Donnelly, "Perspective."

32. Dylan, *Chronicles*, 288.

Bibliography

Arthur, Paul. "No Longer Absolute: Portraiture in American Avant-Garde and Documentary Films of the Sixties." In *Rites of Realism: Essays on Corporeal Cinema*, edited by Ivone Margulies, 93–118. Durham, NC: Duke University Press, 2003.

Baez, Joan. *And a Voice to Sing With: My Story*. New York: Summit Books, 1987.

Banauch, Eugen. "Refractions of Bob Dylan: An Introduction." In *Refractions of Bob Dylan: Cultural Appropriations of an American Icon*, edited by Eugen Banauch, 3–9. Manchester, UK: Manchester University Press, 2015.

Banauch, Eugen, ed. *Refractions of Bob Dylan: Cultural Appropriations of an American Icon*. Manchester, UK: Manchester University Press, 2015.

Bartholomew, Mark, and John Tehranian. "The Changing Landscape of Trademark Law in Tinseltown: From *Debbie Does Dallas* to *The Hangover*." In *Hollywood and the Law*, edited by Paul McDonald, Emily Carman, Eric Hoyt, and Philip Drake, 47–68. London: BFI, 2015.

Bellamy, Jason, and Ed Howard. "The Conversations: Todd Haynes." *Slant Magazine*, August 16, 2010. https://www.slantmagazine.com/film/the-conversations-todd-haynes/.

Belloni, Matthew. "Judge: 'Deep Throat' Owners Can't Stop 'Lovelace' Release." *Hollywood Reporter*, August 7, 2013. https://www.hollywoodreporter.com/business/business-news/judge-deep-throat-owners-cant-602020/.

Bingham, Dennis. *Whose Lives Are They Anyway? The Biopic as Contemporary Film Genre*. New Brunswick, NJ: Rutgers University Press, 2010.

Boddy, William. *Fifties Television: The Industry and Its Critics.* Urbana: University of Illinois Press, 1990. Reprint edition, 1993.

Caldwell, John Thornton. "Independent Television Service." In *The Encyclopedia of Television*, 2nd ed., vol. 1, edited by Horace Newcomb, 1172–1173. New York: Fitzroy Dearborn, 2004.

Coley, Rob. "'I Don't Believe You. . . . You're a Liar': The Fabulatory Function of Bob Dylan." In *Refractions of Bob Dylan: Cultural Appropriations of an American Icon*, edited by Eugen Banauch, 83–97. Manchester, UK: Manchester University Press, 2015.

Cott, Jonathan. "Bob Dylan as Filmmaker: 'I'm Sure of My Dream Self. I Live in My Dreams.'" *Rolling Stone*, January 26, 1978. https://www.rollingstone.com/music/music-news/bob-dylan -as-filmmaker-im-sure-of-my-dream-self-i-live-in-my-dreams -88435/.

Crimp, Douglas. *"Our Kind of Movie": The Films of Andy Warhol.* Cambridge, MA: MIT Press, 2012.

Curwood, Steve. "An Afternoon with Pete Seeger." *Living on Earth*, April 17, 1998. https://www.loe.org/shows/segments .html?programID=19-P13-00031&segmentID=4.

Davis, Nick. "Bringing It All Back Home, or Feminist Suppositions on a Film Concerning Dylan." In *Reframing Todd Haynes: Feminism's Indelible Mark*, edited by Theresa L. Geller and Julia Leyda, 299–316. Durham, NC: Duke University Press, 2022.

D'Cruz, Carolyn, and Glenn D'Cruz. "'Even the Ghost Was More than One Person': Hauntology and Authenticity in Todd Haynes's *I'm Not There*." *Film-Philosophy* 17, no. 1 (2013): 315–330.

DeAngelis, Michael. "There and 'Not There': Todd Haynes and the Queering of Genre." *Celebrity Studies* 8, no. 3 (2017): 578–592.

Decherney, Peter. *Hollywood's Copyright Wars: From Edison to the Internet.* New York: Columbia University Press, 2012.

Decherney, Peter. "One Law to Rule Them All: Copyright Goes

Hollywood." In *Hollywood and the Law*, edited by Paul McDonald, Emily Carman, Eric Hoyt, and Philip Drake, 23–46. London: BFI, 2015.

DeCurtis, Anthony. *Lou Reed: A Life*. New York: Back Bay Books, 2017.

Denning, Michael. "Bob Dylan and Rolling Thunder." In *The Cambridge Companion to Bob Dylan*, edited by Kevin J. H. Dettmar, 28–41. New York: Cambridge University Press, 2009.

Doherty, Thomas. *Hollywood's Censor: Joseph I. Breen and the Production Code Administration*. New York: Columbia University Press, 2007.

Dyer, Richard. *Pastiche*. New York: Routledge, 2007.

Dylan, Bob. *Chronicles: Volume 1*. New York: Simon & Schuster, 2004.

Dylan, Bob. *Tarantula*. New York: St. Martin's Press, 1971. Reprint edition, 1994.

Ebert, Roger. "*Masked and Anonymous*." In *Roger Ebert's Movie Yearbook 2006*, 433–434. Kansas City, MO: Andrews McMeel Publishing, 2006.

Gates, David. "Dylan Revisited." In *Studio A: The Bob Dylan Reader*, edited by Benjamin Hedin, 235–243. New York: W. W. Norton, 2004.

Geiger, John L., and Howard Suber. *Creativity and Copyright: Legal Essentials for Screenwriters and Creative Artists*. Oakland: University of California Press, 2019.

Gray, Michael. "'Rearrange Their Faces and Give Them All Another Name': On Bob Dylan and *I'm Not There*." *Sight and Sound*, January 2008. https://www.bfi.org.uk/sight-and-sound/features/im-not-there-todd-haynes-homage-bob-dylan.

Grierson, Tim. "Tim Robbins Is Asking You to Pirate 'Bob Roberts' Before the Election." *MEL Magazine*, October 12, 2020, https://melmagazine.com/en-us/story/tim-robbins-interview-bob-roberts-movie-download.

Guthrie, Woody. *Roll on Columbia: The Columbia River Collection*. New York: Sing Out Publications, 1991.

Hajdu, David. *Positively 4th Street: The Lives and Times of Joan Baez, Bob Dylan, Mimi Baez Fariña, and Richard Fariña.* New York: Farrar, Straus and Giroux, 2001.

Hall, Jeanne. "'Don't You Ever Just Watch?' American Cinema Verité and *Dont Look Back*." In *Documenting the Documentary: Close Readings of Documentary Film and Video*, edited by Barry Keith Grant and Jeannette Sloniowski, 223–237. Detroit: Wayne State University Press, 1998.

Hanley, David. "Todd Haynes, *I'm Not There*, and the Postmodern Biopic." *Offscreen* 20, no. 4 (April 2016). https://offscreen.com /view/todd-haynes-im-not-there-and-the-postmodern-biopic.

Hawkins, Joan. "Now Is the Time of the Assassins." In *The Cinema of Todd Haynes: All That Heaven Allows*, edited by James Morrison, 25–31. London: Wallflower Press, 2007.

Haynes, Todd. "*I'm Not There*: Developing Dylan." In Christine Vachon with Austin Bunn, *A Killer Life: How an Independent Film Producer Survives Deals and Disasters in Hollywood and Beyond*, 192–196. Montclair, NJ: Limelight Editions, 2007.

Haynes, Todd. "Three Screenplays: An Introduction." In *Far from Heaven, Safe, and Superstar: Three Screenplays*, vii–xii. New York: Grove Press, 2003.

Hentoff, Nat. "Bob Dylan: The *Playboy* Interview." In *Bob Dylan: The Essential Interviews*, edited by Jonathan Cott, 99–118. New York: Wenner Books, 2007.

Hoyt, Eric, Paul McDonald, Emily Carman, and Philip Drake. "Introduction: On the Legal Lives of Hollywood." In *Hollywood and the Law*, edited by Paul McDonald, Emily Carman, Eric Hoyt, and Philip Drake, 1–20. London: BFI, 2015.

"I Am My Words." *Newsweek*, November 4, 1963, 94–95.

Jameson, Fredric. "Postmodernism and Consumer Society." In *The Anti-Aesthetic: Essays on Postmodern Culture*, edited by Hal Foster, 11–125. Port Townsend, WA: Bay Press, 1983.

Jones, Kent. "Chaos, Clocks, Juxtapositions." *The Nation*, December 6, 2007. https://www.thenation.com/article/archive/chaos -clocks-juxtapositions/.

Juhasz, Alexandra, and Jesse Lerner. "Phony Definitions and

Troubling Taxonomies of the Fake Documentary." In *F Is for Phony: Fake Documentary and Truth's Undoing*, edited by Alexandra Juhasz and Jesse Lerner, 1–35. Minneapolis: University of Minnesota Press, 2006.

Kael, Pauline. "The Calvary Gig." In *When the Lights Go Down*, 397–401. New York: Holt, Rinehart and Winston, 1980.

Kael, Pauline. "What's Wrong with This Picture?" In *Movie Love: Complete Reviews, 1988–1991*, 12–22. New York: Dutton, 1991.

Kahana, Jonathan. *Intelligence Work: The Politics of American Documentary*. New York: Columbia University Press, 2008.

Kaufman, Will. *Mapping Woody Guthrie*. Norman: University of Oklahoma Press, 2019.

Kornhaber, Spencer. "Bob Dylan Cheats Again?" *Atlantic*, June 14, 2017. https://www.theatlantic.com/entertainment/archive/2017/06/bob-dylan-nobel-spark-notes-plagarism/530283/.

Landy, Marcia. "Storytelling and Information in Todd Haynes' Films." In *The Cinema of Todd Haynes: All That Heaven Allows*, edited by James Morrison, 7–24. London: Wallflower Press, 2007.

Lane, Anthony. "Tangled Up." *New Yorker*, November 18, 2007. https://www.newyorker.com/magazine/2007/11/26/tangled-up.

Latham, Sean. "Songwriting." In *The World of Bob Dylan*, edited by Sean Latham, 31–45. New York: Cambridge University Press, 2021.

Lebow, Alisa. "Faking What? Making a Mockery of Documentary." In *F Is for Phony: Fake Documentary and Truth's Undoing*, edited by Alexandra Juhasz and Jesse Lerner, 223–237. Minneapolis: University of Minnesota Press, 2006.

Levy, Emanuel. *Gay Directors, Gay Films? Pedro Almodóvar, Terence Davies, Todd Haynes, Gus Van Sant, John Waters*. New York: Columbia University Press, 2015.

Lott, Eric. "*Love and Theft*." In *The Cambridge Companion to Bob Dylan*, edited by Kevin J. H. Dettmar, 167–173. New York: Cambridge University Press, 2009.

Lyotard, Jean-François. "Defining the Postmodern." In *The*

Cultural Studies Reader, 2nd ed., edited by Simon During,
142–145. New York: Routledge, 1993.

MacDonald, Scott. "From Underground to Multiplex: An Interview with Todd Haynes." *Film Quarterly* (Spring 2009):
54–64.

Maddaus, Gene. "Lionsgate Acquires Bulk of Weinstein Film
Library in Spyglass Deal," *Variety*, July 15, 2021. https://
variety.com/2021/film/news/lionsgate-weinstein-co-library
-spyglass-media-1235021200/.

Mann, Denise. *Hollywood Independents: The Postwar Talent
Takeover*. Minneapolis: University of Minnesota Press, 2008.

Marcus, Greil. *Bob Dylan by Greil Marcus: Writings, 1968–2010*.
New York: PublicAffairs, 2010.

Marcus, Greil. "Bob Dylan Times Six: An Interview with 'I'm
Not There' Director Todd Haynes." *Rolling Stone*, November
29, 2007. https://www.rollingstone.com/tv-movies/tv-movie
-news/bob-dylan-times-six-an-interview-with-im-not-there
-director-todd-haynes-67251/.

Marcus, Greil. *The Old, Weird America: The World of Bob Dylan's
Basement Tapes*. New York: Picador, 2011.

Matloff, Jason. "Todd Haynes Takes on Bob Dylan." *MovieMaker*,
November 18, 2007. https://www.moviemaker.com/im-not
-there-todd-haynes-20080122/.

McCarron, Andrew. "Christianity: An Exegesis of *Modern Times*."
In *The World of Bob Dylan*, edited by Sean Latham, 226–236.
New York: Cambridge University Press, 2021.

Mellers, Wilfrid. *A Darker Shade of Pale: A Backdrop to Bob
Dylan*. London: Faber and Faber, 1984.

Millman, Ethan. "Bob Dylan Sells All Recorded Rights to Sony
Music." *Rolling Stone*, January 24, 2022. https://www
.rollingstone.com/music/music-news/bob-dyan-sells-masters
-sony-music-1289763/.

Moverman, Oren. "Superstardust: Talking Glam with Todd
Haynes." In *Velvet Goldmine: A Screenplay by Todd Haynes*,
ix–xxxiii. New York: Miramax Books, 1998.

Moyn, Samuel. *Humane: How the United States Abandoned Peace and Reinvented War*. New York: Farrar, Straus and Giroux, 2021.

Packer, John R., and Mellette. "DISCourse." *Hollywood Studio Magazine*, March 1971, 14.

Paquette, Danielle. "Bob Dylan: 'Wussies and Pussies' Complain about Plagiarism." *The Wrap*, September 12, 2012. https://www.thewrap.com/wussies-and-pussies-complain-about-plagiarism-says-bob-dylan-new-interview-56181/.

Patterson, Lyman Ray. *Copyright in Historical Perspective*. Nashville, TN: Vanderbilt University Press, 1968.

Phillips, Michael. "For 'Carol,' Director Todd Haynes Dug Deep." *Chicago Tribune*, December 17, 2015. https://www.chicagotribune.com/entertainment/movies/ct-todd-haynes-mov-1218-20151217-column.html.

Pichaske, David. *Song of the North Country: A Midwest Framework to the Songs of Bob Dylan*. New York: Continuum, 2010.

Poague, Leland. *Another Frank Capra*. New York: Cambridge University Press, 1994.

Porton, Richard. "The Many Faces of Bob Dylan: An Interview with Todd Haynes." In *Todd Haynes: Interviews*, edited by Julia Leyda, 130–137. Jackson: University Press of Mississippi, 2014.

Prigge, Matt. "It Ain't Me Babe." In *Todd Haynes: Interviews*, edited by Julia Leyda, 149–151. Jackson: University Press of Mississippi, 2014.

Rich, B. Ruby. *New Queer Cinema: The Director's Cut*. Durham, NC: Duke University Press, 2013.

Rogovoy, Seth. *Bob Dylan: Prophet, Mystic, Poet*. New York: Scribner, 2009.

Rosenbaum, Jonathan. "Allusion Profusion." In *Movies as Politics* by Jonathan Rosenbaum, 171–178. Berkeley: University of California Press, 1997.

Rothkopf, Joshua. "Todd Haynes on 30 Years of New Queer Cinema: 'We Were Trying to Make Sense of an Incredibly Scary Time.'" *Entertainment Weekly*, June 30, 2022. https://ew.com/movies/todd-haynes-on-30-years-of-new-queer-cinema/.

Scaduto, Anthony. *Bob Dylan*. New York: Grosset & Dunlap, 1971.

Schlafly, Phyllis. "Fads and Follies in Public Schools." *The Phyllis Schlafly Report*, March 2003. https://eagleforum.org/psr/2003/mar03/psrmar03.shtml.

Schlotterbeck, Jesse. "*I'm Not There*: Transcendent Thanatography." In *The Biopic in Contemporary Film Culture*, edited by Tom Brown and Belén Vidal, 227–242. London: Routledge, 2013.

Scobie, Stephen. "Plagiarism, Bob, Jean-Luc and Me." In *Refractions of Bob Dylan: Cultural Appropriations of an American Icon*, edited by Eugen Banauch, 188–204. Manchester, UK: Manchester University Press, 2015.

Silberg, Jon. "Deconstructing Bob Dylan." *American Cinematographer* 88, no. 11 (November 2007): 38–51.

Smith, Earl Hobson. *Stephen Foster; Or, Weep No More My Lady: A Biographical Play on the Life of Stephen Collins Foster, Father of American Folk Songs*. Knoxville, TN: The Foster Players, 1926.

Smith, Jacob. "A Town Called Riddle: Excavating Todd Haynes's *I'm Not There*." *Screen* 51, no. 1 (Spring 2010): 71–78.

Sounes, Howard. *Down the Highway: The Life of Bob Dylan*. New York: Grove Press, 2011.

Stereogum. "*Factory Girl* Defaming Dylan?" *Stereogum*, December 14, 2006. https://www.stereogum.com/4161/factory_girl_defaming_dylan/news/.

Sullivan, Robert. "This Is Not a Bob Dylan Movie." *New York Times Magazine*, October 7, 2007. https://www.nytimes.com/2007/10/07/magazine/07Haynes.html.

Tsika, Noah. "'I Have My Choice': *Behind Every Good Man* (1967) and the Black Queer Subject in American Nontheatrical Film." In *Screening Race in American Nontheatrical Film*, edited by Allyson Nadia Field and Marsha Gordon, 194–216. Durham, NC: Duke University Press, 2019.

Tsika, Noah. *Screening the Police: Film and Law Enforcement in the United States*. New York: Oxford University Press, 2021.

Vachon, Christine, with Austin Bunn. *A Killer Life: How an Independent Film Producer Survives Deals and Disasters in*

Hollywood and Beyond. Montclair, NJ: Limelight Editions, 2007.

White, Patricia. "Lesbian Reverie: *Carol* in History and Fantasy." In *Reframing Todd Haynes: Feminism's Indelible Mark*, edited by Theresa L. Geller and Julia Leyda, 31–50. Durham, NC: Duke University Press, 2022.

White, Rob. *Todd Haynes*. Urbana: University of Illinois Press, 2013.

Wilentz, Sean. *Bob Dylan in America*. New York: Anchor Books, 2011.

Wilkins, Kim. "'I Don't Know Who I Am Most of the Time': Constructed Identity in Todd Haynes' *I'm Not There*." *Film Criticism*, February 2017. https://quod.lib.umich.edu/f/fc/13761232.0041.103?view=text;rgn=main.

Willman, Chris. "Ronee Blakley Remembers Bob Dylan's Rolling Thunder Revue: 'We Were Delirious.'" *Variety*, June 14, 2019. https://variety.com/2019/music/news/ronee-blakley-interview-rolling-thunder-revue-1203243802/.

Wyatt, Justin. *Poison*. Trowbridge, UK: Flicks Books, 1998.

Yaffe, David. *Bob Dylan: Like a Complete Unknown*. New Haven, CT: Yale University Press, 2011.

Yaffe, David. *Reckless Daughter: A Portrait of Joni Mitchell*. New York: Sarah Crichton Books, 2017.

Yuan, Jada. "The Freewheelin' Hayden." *New York*, February 2, 2007. https://nymag.com/news/intelligencer/27368/.

Zimmer, Ben. "The Delights of Parsing the Beatles' Most Non-sensical Song." *Atlantic*, November 24, 2017. https://www.theatlantic.com/entertainment/archive/2017/11/i-am-the-walrus-50-years-later/546698/.

Index